Fuchsias

Step by Step to Growing Success

George Bartlett

CROWOOD GUIDES

GARDENING

First published in 1990 by
The Crowood Press Ltd
Ramsbury, Marlborough
Wiltshire SN8 2HR

© The Crowood Press Ltd 1990 and 1996

Revised edition 1996

British Library Cataloguing-in-Publication Data

A catalogue record for this book is available from the British Library.

ISBN 1 85223 971 9

Line-drawings by Claire Upsdale-Jones.

Photograph previous page: 'Midwinter' requires a shaded position to thrive.

Picture Credits

All photographs by George Bartlett except for those on the following pages: 8, 14 (upper), 21 (left), 25 (lower), 35, 49, 54, 59, 64, 87, 101 (upper left), 107 (left), 109 (right), 111 (left), 112 (lower right), 119 (upper and lower), 120 (left) (Sue Atkinson); 15, 95, 97 (right), 124, 126 (Dave Pike).

Typeset and designed by
D & N Publishing
Ramsbury, Marlborough
Wiltshire SN8 2HR

Typeface used: Plantin.

Imagesetting by Dorwyn Ltd, Chichester.

Printed in Hong Kong by Paramount Printing Co. Ltd.

Contents

Introduction

Although I have been growing fuchsias since 1966 I often wonder whether a 'health warning' ought to be given as an introduction to any book on the subject. The problem is that, once you embark upon the journey of fuchsia growing, it is extremely hard to give it up. Addiction might be too strong a word to use, but certainly once the 'bug' has bitten it will only be with considerable difficulty that a cure can be effected. To say that fuchsia growers become fanatical would be incorrect, but there is always the temptation to grow just a few more and before long all other horticultural interests are pushed to one side.

Why is there so much interest in this one genus of plants? What is the fascination with a simple flower like the fuchsia? The last question probably gives us a clue to the answer – simplicity. The fuchsia is simple in two ways – in its shape and form, and in its cultivation. Those who have had the pleasure of seeing the hedges of fuchsias growing wild in Ireland or in the west of England long remember the way in which they seem to glow in the sunlight. It is only when a closer examination is made of this mass of red and purple that each individual flower reveals its simplicity. As to their cultivation – the other reason for their popularity – there is nothing very difficult about growing fuchsias. They can be grown in many different ways and used for many different purposes. There are many different cultivars to choose from, and their varying sizes, colour and form give a perpetual kaleidoscope from which

it is difficult to detach your self. Fuchsias are easy to grow and to propagate. they can be grown in all types of conditions, and they will usually do well whatever we do to them. There is no one set of rules which must be obeyed in order to produce a beautiful plant – rules, if made, can be broken and yet still the flowers shake their heads and continue to flourish.

Within this book I have attempted to pass on some of the enthusiasm I have for the fuchsia, and tried to lead the novice along a path which will ensure better than moderate success. I hope that with the beautiful pictures and line-drawings you will be encouraged to grow more of my favourite plants and will want to become involved in those societies which concentrate on promoting the growing of fuchsias.

If, as a result of the success I am sure you will achieve, you wish to become involved with growing plants to be seen on the show benches then I wish you all good luck. My main object, though, is to encourage you to grow your plants for fun and to enjoy growing them. You can brighten the area where you live with a mass of glorious fuchsia blooms and, by passing on pieces of plants for propagation, encourage your neighbours to do the same.

I am certainly grateful to have the opportunity to share my enthusiasm and fun with you.

George Bartlett

'Sandboy', one of the few fuchsias that may keep its buds indoors.

CHAPTER 1

Beginning

CHOOSING YOUR FUCHSIAS

There are so many cultivars from which one can choose that it is perhaps a little difficult to decide which plants to select. Bearing in mind that there are in excess of 8,000 cultivars (perhaps a rather conservative estimate) already listed, then some means of selectively choosing might be called for. Many leading growers concentrate on those plants which, as a result of their naturally symmetrical habits, make good show plants. Such growers will grow a large number of a few differing cultivars.

Those growers whose main objective is to produce something of beauty for their own personal enjoyment can hunt through the catalogues for those which strike a chord. Many growers enjoy the classical simplicity of the single-flowered cultivars whereas other prefer the larger double flowers. Catalogues will always indicate the size of the flower but please bear in mind that the larger the flower the fewer flowers one can expect to be produced.

Another section of the catalogue which might be of interest, and would make an excellent 'collection' in its own right, is the section devoted to *triphylla*-type hybrids. Such plants are always very eye catching with their long tubular flowers and the (usually) purple sheen to the reverse of the leaves; they are perhaps not the easiest to grow, but are very satisfying when success is achieved.

Another group of plants which will make a good collection is the species. With this group we are really going back to our roots as it is from the species that all our modern cultivars have emanated. There are approximately 102 different species, not all, unfortunately, available commercially; those that are available vary from the 'easy to grow' to the 'downright impossible'. Species have in

Magellanica-*type flower*

Semi-double *flower*

Double *flower*

Triphylla-*type flowers*

The triphylla-*type 'Fred Swales' is easy to grow and versatile in that it can be grown as an upright bush or basket subject, or trained as a standard.*

recent years become more popular but growing them is still somewhat of a specialist hobby.

Much easier, and always very eye catching, are the plants which are grown for their foliage rather than for their flowers. Planted in the hardy border they can add considerable colour during the duller weeks of the year when one season is about to end and another has not yet started. Again it will be necessary to hunt through the catalogues for those that will give you the leaf colouring you are seeking.

Recently I have been toying with the idea of gathering together plants which have been raised by specific hybridists. Such groups of fuchsias will be rather limited in numbers but one can build up a very 'select' collection quite easily. If you are in the fortunate position of knowing the raiser and perhaps those after whom the plants have been named then the feeling of personal involvement is even greater.

Finally, how about collecting plants which were raised or introduced in a certain year – perhaps one that has special significance for you. Some research

'Tom West' is often grown primarily for its beautiful foliage.

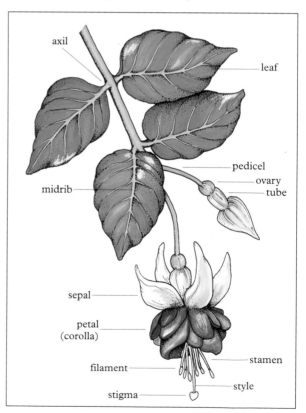

The parts of the fuchsia stem and flower.

will be necessary in order to find the plants but surely that is what a hobby is all about.

I probably will get into trouble with some sections of the fuchsia-growing fraternity for suggesting that fuchsias are items for 'collecting'. The advice generally given is to grow a few plants to the best of your ability, which is the approach most likely to give satisfaction. I suppose we are all guilty of growing far too many – and perhaps suggesting that you build

'Billy Green', floriferous and easy to grow, is an ideal cultivar for the new enthusiast.

STARTING A COLLECTION

If you are just starting a collection it might be a good idea to visit a local show or a fuchsia nursery to see the plants in flower. You might discover that you have a particular liking for one type or colour, or perhaps a style of growth. Whatever it is that catches your imagination, do not obtain too many immediately. Concentrate on perhaps a dozen or twenty, and grow a number of each variety in as many different ways as you can. Get to know their idiosyncrasies and the type of growth they like to produce – for example, those which are lax in growth will make good basket material, and certain others will grow well into the standard form.

Keep a diary at the very start of your fuchsia collecting, listing the names of your plants and their particular requirements. It is surprising how plants vary in the length of time from the final 'stopping' to the flowering date. If you become show-orientated, this information will be vital to you to ensure that your plants are in full bloom for the important day. When visiting shows, take your diary with you and make lists of those plants that you have admired, and possibly the names (and addresses if available) of the growers.

A maximum of twenty varieties would be ideal when first starting to grow – although you won't keep to that number it is a starting point. For ease of growing and success being almost assured, try the following:

Auntie Jinks, Billy Green, Border Queen, Cloverdale Pearl, Garden News, Herald, Joy Patmore, Margaret Brown, Marinka, Mieke Meursing, Phyllis, Royal Velvet, Snowcap, Swingtime, Tennessee Waltz, Thalia, Tom Thumb, Tom West, Westminster Chimes, and Winston Churchill.

Within this personal collection, I have tried to include those with single flowers, those with double flowers, those suitable for the garden and those suitable for hanging baskets.

---

up 'thematic' collections will encourage you to do just that. My intention, however, is to encourage you and perhaps lead you along the path which will bring success; if, en route, more plants are acquired than will comfortably fit into a bulging greenhouse or garden, then so be it. I know there will always be the temptation to purchase just one more – because of its name or simply because you fell in love with the shape and colour of the flower.

OBTAINING YOUR FIRST PLANT

From a Friend

The greatest number of converts to the pleasure of growing fuchsias probably come about as a result of friendship. One of the fuchsia's main attributes is its ability to create a new plant from a piece detached from an existing plant. Growers of fuchsias rapidly realize just how easy it is to 'root' cuttings, and many new plants are produced and then passed on to friends. The motto of the British Fuchsia Society is 'Fuchsia folk are friendly folk', but perhaps it is the flower itself which is the friendlier!

From a Shop

From early spring onwards fuchsia plants, many in full flower, go on offer in shops. Are plants bought early in the year good buys? Much will depend upon the conditions available to you as to whether plants should be bought in, say, early or mid-spring, but in general you should avoid buying any fuchsia plant which is in flower at so early a date. Fuchsias should not really be in flower until the beginning of mid-summer, and some think that even this is rather early. So, how do the growers of these flowering plants manage to produce them so early in the year? What special treatment is necessary and is it possible for the ordinary 'man in the street' to emulate these conditions? In order to flower, a fuchsia needs to be a mature plant and needs to have been living in 'short night' conditions. To ensure the plant's maturity, considerable heat and light are given to it early in the year – during the winter in fact. To encourage flowering, the length of the 'night' is shortened by using lighting, and the plants grow, therefore, in ideal but false conditions. It is difficult to reproduce such conditions, and many of the willing buyers will find these plants lose their flowers and drop their buds soon after being placed in their new quarters.

So, should you buy from shops? Of course – many excellent plants are available – but do leave your buying of fuchsias until they are correctly in season, that is, from mid-summer onwards. That way you will be able to give them the type of conditions in which they will thrive.

In the spring it is also possible to purchase from shops young rooted cuttings, or well-grown young plants which are not yet showing buds. These, especially if they are correctly named, are often excellent buys and are to be recommended. Such plants can be used in many different ways – in the garden, in pots, in troughs, in patio tubs or in baskets. In fact, if you have greenhouse conditions, early spring is an excellent time of the year to buy young plants from shops and garden centres, but do choose them carefully.

From a Nursery

Without doubt the best way to purchase plants is by choosing them at a specialist fuchsia nursery – you will probably find the names of those local to you by examining the pages of gardening papers. You will be able to make your selection from a vast number of clearly-named plants, and you will also be able to decide, especially if you obtain a copy of the nursery catalogue before your visit, precisely which plants you wish to acquire and the purpose for which you wish to grow them. In most nurseries the plants will be set out in alphabetical order and there will be long rows of individual cultivars. You will, therefore, have the opportunity to choose the strongest of the cultivars.

'Viva Ireland', an excellent bedding subject, which will also provide a fine display in the hanging container.

You should be warned, however, that there will be great temptation to buy many more plants than you originally intended, and you will probably have to be very firm with yourself. Have a list prepared well in advance – decide how many of each cultivar you will require, remembering that a basket will look much better if it contains a number of the same cultivar. You might even consider sending your list to the nursery in advance of your visit so that they can be ready for you on arrival. Although this will rob you of the opportunity to choose the strongest for yourself, you will probably find that the nurseryman will select those he considers the best for you.

At nurseries it is also possible to choose between 'rooted cuttings' and 'small plants'. The former will need extra care once you get them home, but they will be slightly cheaper. Usually it is better to go for the latter – young plants which will probably already have been 'stopped', and will thus be producing their first branches.

Perhaps the most important advantage of visiting a nursery to buy your plants is the opportunity you have to talk to the person who has raised them. A discussion (always freely and willingly given in nurseries), will tell you the type of compost that has

'Silver Anniversary' is useful for the basket, but also makes a very striking bush.

been used, and give you advice on how to get the best from the growing plants. Also, it is possible to visit such nurseries from January onwards, so, provided you have the right conditions at home, you will have a head start with your young plants. Rooted cuttings bought in late winter and early spring will produce fine flowering specimens growing in 5–6in (13–15cm) pots from mid-summer onwards. Plants will also have achieved the right type of growth for planting out in the garden from the beginning of June.

Through the Post

If you glance through the gardening publications you will see a vast number of addresses from which it is possible to obtain young fuchsia plants. Many of the descriptions given, and the prices charged, will encourage growers to send for the plants or collections offered, but this is one method of buying which should be considered carefully – not because the quality of goods on offer is likely to be poor, but because any young plants enclosed in a box, completely without light and moisture for a number of

'Margaret Pilkington'.

The full, double blooms of 'Southgate'. This cultivar can be grown as a bush or as a basket subject.

days, are likely to suffer a setback. Do not be tempted to go for the cheapest plants or collections on offer – they are usually cheaper because the quality of the packing is inferior. Many of the specialist fuchsia nurseries send their plants in specially-designed boxes, and very often by rail. Such plants usually arrive in excellent condition.

My honest opinion would be, buy through the post if you must, but please remember that your plants will need very careful attention when they arrive. Dissatisfaction with the quality of the goods received should always be reported back immediately to the nursery concerned. Delays, often not of their making, are frequently the cause of the dissatisfaction.

FIRST STEPS

Having obtained your very first plant, the anxious question arises as to what you should now do with it. There can be no simple answer to this, as much will depend upon the size of the plant, the type of pot in which it is growing, and the time of the year.

Mail-ordered Cuttings

Very often when you receive small rooted cuttings through the post they will be wrapped in moist paper, as it is less costly to send them this way than by including the pot and a quantity of compost. Whether the cutting is in a pot or in paper, it should be dealt with in the same way. Consider always that the plants, since rooting, have received a traumatic shock, and treat them very carefully indeed.

For potting your cuttings, peat-based composts are well balanced, with sufficient nutritional value to keep your plants happy for a few weeks, and they are often more reliable than loam-based composts. However, if you like using a loam-based compost, and can guarantee getting a good fresh supply, it will be no problem – fuchsias will grow quite happily in whatever compost you choose.

Assuming your cuttings are obtained during the spring, the temperature in which the young plants are placed is critical – the ideal will be in the vicinity of 50°F (10°C). At this type of temperature the young plants will start to grow away quite rapidly. If you are caring for the cuttings in a greenhouse,

POTTING MAIL-ORDERED CUTTINGS STEP-BY-STEP

You will need:

❀ Small pots, preferably no larger than 3in (7.5cm) in diameter; 2½in (6cm) pots are ideal

❀ 1 smaller pot in which each cutting's rootball will fit snugly

❀ A good peat-based compost (or loam based if your prefer)

❀ Plastic labels

❀ Scissors

❀ Fine-rose watering can

❀ Newspaper or horticultural fleece

Before starting, write the names of the cuttings on the plastic labels with a marker or pencil.

1. Remove the new cuttings from the box, one at a time, and examine each for any obvious signs of damage or disease. Then carefully remove the paper and any old compost that may still be adhering to the roots. Spread the young white roots out and use the scissors to cut away any that are damaged or appear brown in colour.

2. Place each prepared cutting in close proximity to its label so that there is no possibility of the cuttings becoming mixed up.

POTTING MAIL-ORDERED CUTTINGS STEP-BY-STEP

3. Deal with each young cutting one at a time: take a pot and place a small quantity of your compost in the base. Place the smaller pot on top of the compost and then fill both this and the new pot. Tap the new pot on the bench to settle the compost, and then remove the smaller pot; its depression will remain in the compost. Take a cutting and gently separate its roots. Holding the cutting over the pot with the roots spread out in the depression, add compost until the roots are covered. Do not firm the compost at all but let it settle around the roots by gently tapping the pot on the table or bench (opposite, bottom).

4. Place the label in the pot, inserting it between the compost and the side of the pot to avoid damaging the roots. Systematically repeat the procedure with each cutting, remembering to label each cutting as soon as it is potted (above).

5. When all the cuttings have been dealt with in this way, place all the potted cuttings on a tray on the window-sill or on the staging of the greenhouse. Gently water the plants with the fine-rose watering can. This watering will firm the compost around the roots of the cuttings (above right).

6. Whether you are growing your plants in the greenhouse or indoors on the window-sill, the young plants will not appreciate dry heat, so keep them fairly cool and protect them from the sun by covering them. Horticultural fleece is ideal for the purpose; otherwise a single sheet of paper is quite satisfactory. This will keep them shaded and will, at the

same time, create a pleasant moist atmosphere which will help to keep the cuttings turgid until the roots begin to draw moisture from the compost. Inspect the cuttings daily; it might be a good idea to give them a gentle overhead spraying with slightly tepid, pure water. After approximately a week, the roots will have started to work their way around the compost and the shading can be removed (above).

Fuchsia cuttings rooting in cellular trays.

and you do not wish to heat the whole of the house to this temperature, it might be as well to provide yourself with a small propagator which can give the necessary temperature and protection. Consideration might also be given to partitioning off a small area of your greenhouse, and heating that to the required temperature. In the early part of the year the essential is to make sure that the plants do not suffer from excessive cold. Below a temperature of 40°F (about 5°C), the young plants will feel decidedly chilly and will not grow.

If the young plants are bought in during early summer, your major cause for concern will be shading from too hot a sun. This is an easy task which can be accomplished by using sheets of newspaper or horticultural fleece.

Young Plants from Nurseries

When good young plants or rooted cuttings are obtained from specialist fuchsia nurseries, it is probably (in fact, almost certain) that each will be growing in its own individual pot, and for this reason the young plant should suffer no setback when you transfer it to your own premises. One word of warning is that if your new acquisitions have been growing in ideal, warm and humid conditions, transfer-

'Tamworth', whose growth is upright, vigorous and bushy, and whose striking flowers are freely produced.

ring them to the back of a cold car could be upsetting. Make preparations before leaving for the nursery to ensure that your purchases will remain snug and warm – a cardboard box insulated with newspapers will help to keep out the cold, as will a seed

Spraying young plants newly obtained from nurseries, rather than watering them, will help to keep the compost moist and the atmosphere humid (above).

A small greenhouse and pot-grown fuchsias.

tray propagator with its plastic dome. Perhaps the most important thing to remember is that once you have purchased your plants you should make all speed to get them home and in the comfort of your own accommodation.

Once home, examine your plants carefully. Leave them in the pots in which they are growing for a week or two, placing them in conditions similar to those in which they were growing in the nursery. Keep them, for a few days at least, in your own propagator so that the humidity surrounding them is fairly high.

TRANSFERRING PLANTS IN PEAT POTS

Do not attempt to remove the peat pot when transferring the plant into a plastic pot. Take a 3½in (9cm) plastic pot, place a small quantity of your compost in the base, stand your well-moistened peat-potted plant on this and completely fill the sides so that the surplus completely covers the peat pot. No part of the peat pot should be visible – if it is, the air will dry the moisture from the peat pot causing it to dry out completely and go hard. Once filled, your new pot should be watered well and should subsequently be kept moister than is usually recommended. By using this method the roots will grow through the peat pot, which will disintegrate fairly quickly and will become part of the compost in your new pot.

'Bornemann's Beste', an upright, vigorous grower.

'Blue Sails', one of the triphylla hybrids. It is a strong grower and, with correct management, will flower profusely for a long period.

Spray them overhead regularly (as opposed to watering them), so that the compost they are in remains just moist. If you have a collection of plants already it is not a bad idea to keep your new ones segregated from the rest for two or three weeks, just in case they have an infection which could be passed on – it is not unknown even for specialist fuchsia nurseries to suffer from the debilitating disease called 'rust'. Any infection on your new plants should become visible within that span of time.

Some fuchsia nurseries root their young plants in peat pots. These pots are excellent, but they do cause some growers (even experienced ones!) anxiety. If you have ever purchased these peat pots you will have read the instructions which advise you to soak the pots thoroughly before using them. This soaking causes the pots to become sufficiently soft for young roots to penetrate the sides. There have been complaints that the peat pots harden and prevent roots from penetrating, but this can only happen when moisture is leached out of the pots, and they become dry. This can be prevented. If you have bought young plants rooted in these pots completely immerse the pots in water, thoroughly soaking them – if you can do this overnight it will be especially beneficial.

CHAPTER 2

Basics

COMPOST

There is no magical compost formula which will guarantee success when growing plants, but we fuchsia growers are lucky, as the needs of the fuchsia are minimal. What type of compost is it therefore best to use? Basically, if you are happy with the type of compost you usually use when growing other pot plants – perhaps John Innes potting or seed composts – and you can guarantee being able to obtain good fresh supplies, use them for your fuchsias. The John Innes formulae have proved very successful over the years, especially when used in conjunction with clay pots. The loam base of this compost is heavier, and with the porosity of clay pots sufficient air will permeate to assist in the aeration of the roots.

Similarly, if you like using the Levington potting composts, and are successful with them, then use them for your fuchsias. These are peat-based composts and will therefore be more suitable when used in conjunction with plastic pots. They are well balanced with regard to fertilizers and your fuchsias will thrive in them.

Arthur Bowers is another of the well-known peat-based composts often used by successful growers. If the consistency of this compost suits your style of growing, use it for your fuchsias.

The Humber Potting Compost is the one I personally use and recommend. It too is a peat-based compost, although it does contain a certain amount of loam and rather more grit than most other similar composts.

If you mix your own compost, and are happy with the results, continue to do so – there is much to be said for this practice, it probably works out slightly cheaper and it does not require a great deal of effort.

However, do not be tempted to use earth from the garden. Many people are, and they are very often disappointed with the results achieved. This is a method not to be recommended, even if you have only one or two plants.

MAKING YOUR OWN COMPOST

Various elements make a compost suitable for fuchsias. Basically, fuchsias require a compost that has the ability to hold moisture and nutrient but that is also well drained. Fuchsias like to have a moistness around their roots but do not want to be standing in a wet mess, so I prefer to err on the side of increasing the drainage of a compost and am prepared to add further sharp sand, grit or perlite.

You will need:

❀ 6 parts peat
❀ 2 parts sharp sand, grit or perlite
❀ Chempak compost mix, readily available from garden supply outlets
❀ Large container, such as a plastic refuse bin.

Simply mix the ingredients together in the large container. If you are mixing more than a small amount, it is a good idea to add the ingredients gradually, mixing them after each addition; otherwise you may find it difficult to blend the ingredients thoroughly.

POTTING

Every gardener must bear in mind that restricting the roots of any plant in a container is completely unnatural. In the garden, or in the wild, the roots are free to roam at will in their search for the nutrients necessary to maintain the vigorous growth of the plant. We must therefore consider the needs of the plant and the desire of those roots to forage. One aspect which is most important is that there can only be growth of the top foliage of any plant if there is movement and growth of the roots. If the roots are restricted and cannot grow, or the source of food within a container has been completely exhausted, the plant will feel threatened and will do what nature intends – that is, produce seeds as quickly as possible to ensure the continuation of the species. To produce its seeds it must first produce its flowers. When that happens, growth of the foliage will slow down or perhaps even stop. Gardeners make use of nature's need to produce seeds to encourage their plants to flower as and when they require.

When considering what type of container to use for your plants, you should look only at those which have drainage holes in the base through which excess water can pass. Fuchsias need a good, well-drained compost so undrained containers will be of little use. The two types of flower pots usually used by growers of fuchsias are made of plastic and clay. When deciding upon which is the better, much depends on the type of compost you prefer to use. A peat-based compost, which tends to dry out more quickly than a loam-based one, will be more suitable with plastic pots. Conversely, a loam-based compost is more appropriate when using the more porous clay pots. Having said that, growers using either type of pot with all types of compost still produce good results, and experience will show the right pot and compost for you.

The size of the pot used will depend a great deal upon the size of the plant and its root formation. A young cutting about 2in (5cm) high would look lost in a 6in (15cm) pot, and the small root system would be surrounded by a great deal of unused compost – it would be rather like putting a young baby in a large double bed! You should get used to planting in pots which will just comfortably take the root system.

Potting plants is an art, and one that improves with practice. A quantity of your fresh compost should be placed in the base of the pot, the rooted cutting held centrally with one hand whilst fresh compost is allowed to trickle around the roots until the pot has been filled. A tap on the bench will settle the compost around the root system, and the task

POTTING ROOTED CUTTINGS

When your cuttings have rooted they should be carefully separated from their compatriots (if more than one have been rooted together), and placed in a pot not exceeding 3in (7.5cm) in diameter. Some growers at this stage wash away all the compost from the roots so that when potted the young plant will be in completely new compost. If the cuttings have been rooted separately there is no need to carry out this task.

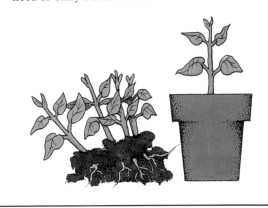

can be completed by watering with the fine rose on the watering can. I would never advise firming the compost around the root system with your fingers or thumbs. Let the watering do the firming for you.

For the compost to be able to 'trickle', it should be just moist in texture. If it is too wet it will be lumpy, and if it is too dry, although it will 'trickle', it will be difficult to moisten later. To test the compost for the right state of moistness take a handful in one hand and squeeze it. If moisture oozes from it, then it is too wet, and if when the hand is opened the compost falls to pieces it is too dry. If it retains the shape of the closed hand and only separates when poked with a finger, then it is correct.

When the pot in which you have placed your young plant has become filled with roots it is time to move your plant into a larger pot. 'Filled with roots', is probably the incorrect thing to say. Examine the rootball regularly by inverting the flower pot and letting the compost and roots rest upon your hand. If fresh young white roots are readily visible through the compost at the sides of the pot, and roots have reached the bottom, then it is time to 'pot on'. Do not wait until the roots are circling the

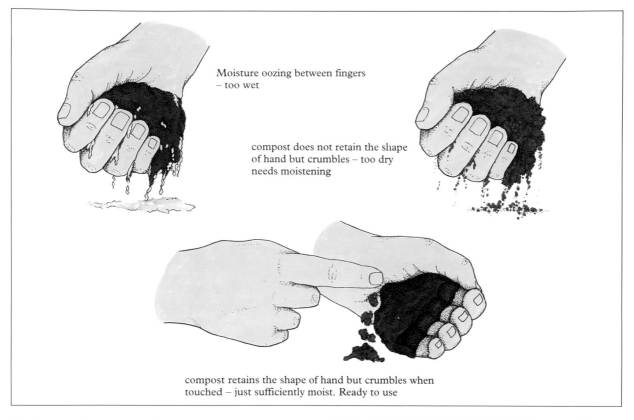

Moisture oozing between fingers
– too wet

compost does not retain the shape
of hand but crumbles – too dry
needs moistening

compost retains the shape of hand but crumbles when
touched – just sufficiently moist. Ready to use

Testing the moisture content of compost.

compost as they will have difficulty later in working through the new compost.

What size pot should you be aiming for in the first season? A cutting taken in February or March should finish up in a pot of either 5in (13cm) or 6in (15cm) in its first season, where it will flower quite happily. Plants which have been over-wintered and which started in 3½in (9cm) pots or even 5in (13cm) pots at the beginning of the season can grow to a much larger size and will probably need 7, 8 or 9in (17.5, 20 or 22.5cm) pots or tubs. Try to get your plant in a pot proportional to its size.

If you are training your plants to grow as standards it is important to keep moving the plants into larger pots so that there is room for the root growth which will encourage top growth. If the pot is full of roots before the required height is reached, the plant, feeling threatened, will start to produce its flower buds and upward growth will cease.

'Piquant Prince'.

POTTING ON STEP-BY-STEP

This simple method of transferring plants from 3in (7.5cm) pots into 4in (10cm) or 5in (13cm) pots saves time and mess, and avoids root disturbance. It also reduces the possibility of getting compost on the lower foliage.

1. Place a small quantity of compost in the base of the new pot. Take another pot of the same size as that in which the plant is currently growing and place it in the new pot on this compost. Using fresh, just moist compost, fill the pot to overflowing and continue to add more compost until the new pot is also full.

2. Tap the new pot on the bench to settle the compost and reveal the rim of the smaller pot. (It is not necessary to firm the compost with your fingers.) Without disturbing the compost, carefully remove the smaller pot to leave its moulded shape on the compost.

3. Carefully remove your plant from its old pot, taking care not to disturb the rootball. Before transferring it, examine the rootball for signs of damage or disease; if any signs are apparent, this should be dealt with before you replant it.

4. Gently drop it into the hole in the new pot. A tap on the bench and the job is completed, without fuss or mess.

'Orange Drops' is ideal for growing as a weeping standard.

There are two reasons why you should go to the trouble of gradually 'potting on' from one pot to another. The first and most obvious is that a very large pot will take up much more room on the window-sill or greenhouse staging early in the season. The second reason (perhaps more important) is that you are regularly giving your plants fresh compost through which their roots can move in search of fresh nutrients. If you give the plant all the compost it will eventually need at one go, many of the nutrients will be washed away during watering, before the roots have an opportunity of reaching them. In this case you would have to start 'feeding' the plants at an earlier stage than is usually necessary.

There is extra effort involved, but the results will justify the additional work. Handling your plants regularly is most important, and there is no better way of finding out if anything is wrong than the process of 're-potting'.

The same method of forming a mould in the new container is extremely useful when you come to make up full or half baskets. In this way the positioning of the plants within the container can be seen before the plants are actually placed in the compost.

WATERING

The subject of the frequency and quantity of watering causes anxiety to many gardeners, but there should be no problem provided a few simple rules are remembered.

When preparing the compost for growing fuchsias, it is a good idea to add additional grit or sharp sand to give extra drainage. Fuchsias do not like

'Happy Wedding day', whose large blooms are freely produced considering their size.

standing with their roots in a soggy, damp, cold compost, so the compost should be moist, as opposed to wet, the rootball should never be allowed to dry out completely, as the roots will shrivel, but if the plant is standing continuously in water the roots will rot and the plant will die.

As to the methods of watering – pouring water on to the top of the compost, or into a saucer, allowing the roots to take up the water they require – either is equally satisfactory. If you water from above (and if your plants are on an indoor window-sill the pots should be standing, to protect the furniture, in a saucer), any excess water that gathers in the saucer should be removed after a few minutes. If you water by filling the saucer in which the plant pot is standing, allow about fifteen minutes for the plant to take up all the moisture it requires and them throw away the excess. Plants growing in a greenhouse may be watered by spraying from above, an excellent method which also allows the plants to take in moisture through the leaves. The difficulty here is in assessing exactly how much water has been given to each plant. It is better to treat each plant individually, filling the pot to the brim with water and allowing it to drain through the roots and out of the drainage hole in the base of the pot. This method is certainly essential when you are feeding the plants each time you water. Remember – *do not allow your plants to be standing permanently in water.*

It does not seem to matter to any great extent whether water is used directly from the public mains or whether rain water is collected. Regularity in applying this moisture is the most important aspect of watering.

You will find that it will not be necessary, in the early part of the year, to water each plant every day, since the lack of warmth in the sun means the extent of evaporation and transpiration will not be so great. However, as the season progresses and the sun rises higher in the sky, it might well be necessary to supply water to your plants once a day, or even more frequently. There can be no rule of thumb laid down, as much will depend upon your own circumstances, but basically the aim will be to maintain a well-drained, moist compost, through which it will be possible to give the essential nutrients to the plants.

'America', whose lax growth makes it a natural choice for the basket or hanging container.

In spite of all the gardener's efforts, there are occasions when the compost within the pots completely dries out, perhaps as a result of a weather change during an absence of a couple of days. Unfortunately the peat-based composts are very difficult to re-moisten by normal watering methods, with the water passing straight through the compost and out of the drainage holes. Compost also tends to shrink away from the edge of the pot so that there is an easy exit for the water down the sides. The only real solution to this problem is to immerse the pot and compost completely in a bucket of water, holding it under the water until the bubbles cease rising to the surface. Remove from the bucket and allow to drain, then after a few minutes repeat the process. After the second 'dunking' the compost is usually completely re-moistened. You can now continue watering in the usual way.

OVERWATERED PLANTS

If your plant is suffering from excessive watering, and the pot feels very heavy when lifted, drastic treatment will be necessary. Remove the plant from the pot and examine the rootball – if it is very wet, speed up the drying-out process by standing the rootball on an inverted pot and allowing it to drain. If the plant does not make a slight recovery after a couple of hours, and the roots visible around the side of the compost look brown – and perhaps the compost as a whole smells – further action is necessary. Remove as much of the old compost as possible and prune away any roots that

are obviously dead or badly damaged. (If the compost is difficult to remove, it may be necessary to run the rootball under the tap for a few seconds or dunk it in a bucket of water.) Repot into fresh compost. Treat such plants as invalids for a few days by placing then in a spot shaded from the direct rays of the sun. You should give no additional water to the rootball, but regular spraying overhead will help to refresh the foliage. After a few days, when the foliage is beginning to look perkier, and the roots are obviously beginning to forage in the new compost, the plant can be returned to its normal place on the bench.

Plants growing in hanging baskets, or in patio tubs and in pots standing outside, are open to the elements (the strong sun and drying winds), and will need very careful regular attention. This factor should be taken into consideration in the first instance when you are deciding upon the methods to be used in growing and displaying your plants. When filled with well-grown plants and containing moist compost, a hanging basket will be quite heavy, difficult to move, and might well need watering *in situ*. Accessibility will therefore be an important consideration. Learn to feel the weight of each plant pot, so that you will be able to tell by feel if the plant needs watering. A light weight with light colouring of the surface of the compost will indicate the need for water. A pot which feels heavy, with dark-coloured compost, will probably not. Get to know your plants. A plant which has dull, lifeless-looking leaves which are drooping will probably be suffering from lack of moisture. Conversely (or perhaps perversely), the same symptoms could indicate an excess of moisture and damage to the root system.

FEEDING

During the course of the season you will need to feed your plants. The compost in which you originally placed your fuchsias will, with the passage of time, and with watering, lose its nutritional value. Fuchsias will benefit considerably from regular feeding, and in fact, they are often considered to be gross feeders. All their nutrition is taken up through the roots or through their leaves, so, although it is possible to sprinkle general dry fertilizers around the base of plants, and leave the rain or the water to dissolve the food and take it to the roots, it is easier to supply foods as liquids. The variety of choice available to us these days is immense, but there are basic guidelines as to what a liquid feed should contain.

Any feed should contain nitrogen (N), phosphates (P) and potash (K), together with minute quantities of trace elements such as magnesium, boron, iron, manganese, copper, zinc and molybdenum. On any packet or bottle of fertilizer that you purchase you will see an analysis of the contents. It is the N, P and K numbers which are important, as it is the quantity of each of these elements which will decide when it is best to use the fertilizer.

The 'N' (nitrogen) stimulates the growth of the foliage and helps to build up a good sturdy plant. It

'Indian Maid' is an excellent basket subject, but will also make a beautiful bush if pinched early.

be suitable for use at the beginning of the season. A feed with 15–15–30 will have a high potash content, and should be used when the plants have reached the size required and you want to encourage the ripening of the wood and flowering.

As to the frequency of feeding and the strength at which it should be applied, you cannot do better than refer to the label on the packet. Do not be tempted to exceed the recommended dose. Nothing is gained by it and in fact a great deal of harm may be done, as serious scorching and damage of the roots may occur if too great a concentration is used. The recommended strength of feed is one level teaspoon of crystals to each gallon (4.5 litres) of water, applied weekly to your plants. For even better results, try reducing the strength to a quarter and use one level teaspoonful to every 4 gallons (18 litres) of water and apply each time the plant is given a drink. Little and often might be best, and this will also get round the problem of remembering when you last fed your plants.

There are many different types of feed available in garden centres and all are equally useful. Make a habit of examining the labels on the bottles or packets and use the one whose formula is best suit-

is, therefore, essential to have a feed containing a fair proportion of this commodity in the early part of the season when the plant is making good, fast, luscious growth.

The 'P' (phosphate) helps to build up a good strong root system, so, again, this chemical is particularly important at the beginning of the growing cycle of the plant.

The 'K' (potash) is vitally important to plants at all times, as it assists in the use of the nitrogen content of the feed, helps to prevent soft, sappy growth, and helps to improve the colour of the flowers. As the season progresses, potash will help to ripen the wood and prepare the plant for flowering.

The analysis you can expect to find on a packet of feeding crystals will always follow the same layout – three numbers (for example, 25–15–15) will refer to the proportions of nitrogen, phosphates and potash, in that order. Therefore, a feed described as 25–15–15 will have a high nitrogen content, and will

'Misty Morn' makes a good container subject.

ed to your needs at that time – high 'N' in the spring, balanced N.P.K. during the main growing season, and high 'K' when flowering is required.

Most of the liquid fertilizers, being very soluble, are also useful for feeding the plant through the leaves (foliar feeding). Although the structure of many leaves prevents a great deal of absorption, this is certainly a valuable means of feeding the plants, especially when they have recently been re-potted and there has been some traumatic disturbance to the root system. Such feeding should only be carried out during the early growing season, and not when young buds are beginning to form, as it is possible for some marking of the buds and resulting flowers to occur.

Regular feeding of your plants is important and can make all the difference between adequate plants and those of which you can be proud.

'Arcadia Gold', a sport of 'Swingtime', has vivid flowers and interesting foliage. It grows well in baskets.

'Brutus' in the summer bed (below).

CHAPTER 3

Increasing your Stock

CUTTINGS

One of the best things about growing fuchsias is the opportunity you have of increasing the number of your plants by taking cuttings. Many, perhaps most, plants can be reproduced by taking cuttings. Some are extremely difficult and need ideal conditions, whereas others will root very readily. Fuchsias come into the second category, and you will find that it is the simplest of operations to persuade a piece of a fuchsia plant to root. I once attended a meeting where the speaker was discussing the methods by which another genus could be persuaded to root; he suddenly threw in the comment, 'Of course you fuchsia growers are lucky; you only have to drop a cutting on a damp floor and it will root!' Perhaps an exaggeration, but certainly close to the truth.

Various things are needed for success in rooting cuttings. First and foremost you will require good stock material. Secondly, you need a propagator and compost, and moistness and warmth, not heat – I am sure that the vast majority of failures that occur are as a result of excessive heat. If you provide good, warm, humid conditions for your young cuttings, they will root in about two to three weeks.

Compost

How do you go about it? First, you need to consider the compost in which cuttings will root. Fuchsia cuttings will in fact root in pure water, as well as moist sand, vermiculite, perlite, or any other substance which will retain moisture. They will therefore root easily in pure peat. You may have been advised that the compost in which the cuttings are initially rooted should contain no nutrient at all. In fact, a mixture of 50 per cent peat and 50

per cent sharp sand, vermiculite or perlite, is often recommended by leading growers and nurserymen. This excellent material will hold moisture, and, with the addition of warmth, roots can be encouraged to form. With that warmth, following the rules of nature, those roots will immediately start foraging for food. If the compost contains no

'Variegated Brenda White' a sport from 'Brenda White'.

The vivid blooms and glossy foliage of 'Red Dragon'.

Containers

The second thing to consider is the type of container in which to root your cuttings. You need something in which a high humidity can be maintained, as you must be sure that, once you have severed the cutting from the parent plant, there will be no wilting or loss of moisture from that cutting before the roots have formed. There are many types of containers available, but you may well find that the cheapest are the most effective.

At the top of the price range are electrically-heated propagators, which are the size of one or two seed trays and have a perspex cover. These are excellent and can be used not only for rooting your fuchsia

coffee jar   jam jar

sweet jar

Types of propagator.

food, the plant, in its anxiety to find nutrients, will form more and more roots to join the frantic search. An excellent root system is therefore built up very quickly. When it has developed sufficiently, and is transferred into a compost containing the essential foods, it will help to build up an excellent plant. For this to work, you must be in the position to pot on your cuttings at the correct time. Failure to do this will result in stunted and woody growth, since you will not have provided the young rooted cutting with the essential nutrients.

I prefer a compost consisting of a mixture of my normal potting compost, with an equal portion of vermiculite. Adding vermiculite reduces the nutritional value of the compost (although there is some present). When they are inserted in this compost and given moisture and warmth, the cuttings root and when they start foraging for food they are successful in finding it. As a result the roots develop, and the plant will start to grow and will remain succulent. The resulting root system might not be as extensive as that developed in pure peat, but it will, nevertheless, be quite adequate.

cuttings, but also for germinating some of those more difficult seeds which require higher temperatures. The one fault with this type of propagator is that they are *too* good, and give too much heat for the successful rooting of fuchsia cuttings. However, you can reduce the heat, so that you have a gentle warmth, by placing a layer of gravel, sand or perlite in the base of the tray. This insulation will also be a means by which a high humidity can be maintained.

Another simple propagator that can be purchases at a reasonable price is a half or full tray unheated propagator, again with a perspex dome. These are excellent as they can be used on a window-sill, and the heat of the room is sufficient to assist the rooting process. Within a half tray sized propagator it is possible to root a considerable number of cuttings at one go, depending upon the size of the cuttings that you take.

As you are looking for some structure which will maintain a humid atmosphere around the cuttings, it is possible, with imagination, to think of many use-ful, and free, types of propagator covers. If you invert a large coffee jar, and stand a small flower pot on the lid, you have the perfect propagator. A large jam jar, again inverted and covering a 3½in (9cm) pot can also be used. Other examples are plastic sweet jars, and plastic bags supported by wires or sticks.

Preparation

When taking a cutting, you are looking for a piece of the plant which you can remove from the parent plant and encourage to root, and it is possible that some pieces will root more easily than others. Given the right conditions, practically any part of the fuchsia plant will form roots, but it is useful to know which parts are most likely to be successful, and which will root the easiest. Without doubt the best cutting material is found at the end of the young shoots. The very end tip of each shoot is referred to as the soft green tip, and in the early part of the year such shoots are easily obtained.

Given the right conditions, almost any part of the fuchsia will form roots.

Before preparing the cutting for insertion into the cutting compost you must have everything ready. Above all, it is important that the cutting, once severed from the parent plant, should not be allowed to wilt. Prepare the compost by placing it in the container and giving it a watering using a fine rose on a watering can. The cuttings can now be prepared. The usual recommendation is that a cutting is removed from the parent by cutting just beneath a leaf node. The bottom leaves are then removed, and ideally you will be left with a cutting about 2in (5cm) long with a growing tip and two pairs of young leaves. Given the right conditions, such a cutting will root well. However, it is not necessary to remove from the plant by cutting below the leaf node – this also removes the small embryo shoots situated in the leaf axils which, if left, will develop into new shoots. I remove a piece of the

---

TYPES OF CUTTINGS

Green tip cuttings are not the only type of cuttings that will root easily. Although they are perhaps the simplest of all, it is fair to say that practically any part of a fuchsia plant can be encouraged to root. Should it be your good fortune to find a branch of one of your plants 'sporting' a flower or leaves of a different colour, you will want to obtain as many cuttings as possible from that branch. The soft green tip will supply just one. However if you look down the stem you will see that there are small shoots appearing at each leaf axil, and these can be used quite satisfactorily. A piece of stem containing leaves can be cut both above and below the leaves and this will provide another cutting. If the shoots further down the branch are slightly longer, it is possible to remove the part containing the leaves and, by carefully slicing down through the piece of stem, two small cuttings will be available.

---

plant by cutting just *above* the leaf node; the length of my cutting will be about 1–1½in (2.5–4cm) and it will consist of a growing tip and one set of leaves.

Having prepared your cutting in either way, gently push it into the compost. If a number of cuttings are placed in the same container, you should water them in, again using a very fine rose on a watering can. This will have the effect of settling the compost around the cuttings. A label bearing the name of the plant from which the cuttings were taken, together with the date upon which the operation was carried out, is inserted, and the whole is covered with its propagator cover.

Conditions and Care

It is now a matter of time before our cuttings will form roots but we must ensure that they are given the right conditions. The propagator can be placed on a window-sill in the house, where the ambient temperature will be sufficient to assist in the formation of roots. Do not, however, place the propagator on a window-sill which is facing towards the sun, as the warmth of the sun shining through the window and the cover of the propagator will create considerable heat, and the cuttings will be killed. A north-facing window is ideal. If you have to use a south-facing one, you will have to provide some form of shading from the sun.

The semi-double 'Icecap' makes an excellent show plant.

PROPAGATION USING A SWEET JAR STEP-BY-STEP

I recommend a sweet jar more than any other container for rooting cuttings: it is easily obtainable, light, and capable of maintaining the humidity that is vital for young cuttings. And of course it has the added advantage that it doesn't cost anything.

Before starting, ensure that the parent plants are well watered in advance so that every part of the plant is completely charged with moisture.

You will need:

❀ A clean sweet jar
❀ A section of modulated tray which will fit inside the sweet jar. (I use the Plantpak trays which have fifty or sixty modules in groups of ten or twelve; a strip of these will fit very nicely through the opening to the jar.)

❀ A supply of just-moist compost (half multi-purpose, half vermiculite)
❀ Plant labels (reduced in size so that they will pass through the jar opening)
❀ A marking pen
❀ A sharp hobby knife
❀ Watering can with a fine rose

1. Fill the modules with compost, which should be light and open, so do not firm it in any way. Using a sharp hobby knife, sever the cutting from the plant by cutting just above the leaf node at the very tip of the branch. (If the leaves are rather large, a portion can be removed so that there is no danger of cuttings overlapping within the propagator.)

PROPAGATION USING A SWEET JAR STEP-BY-STEP

2. Push the cutting gently into the compost so that the next set of leaves is just resting upon the surface. If you are taking individual cuttings from a number of plants, the label should be written and inserted straight away. Do not be tempted to leave this part of the proceedings until later as memory can play nasty tricks.

3. Continue taking cuttings until all the modules in the strip have been filled. The cuttings should now be settled into the compost by giving them a good watering using a fine rose on the watering can.

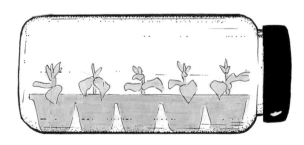

4. The strip of modules containing the cuttings can now be placed inside the sweet jar and the lid screwed on.

5. The propagator should be placed in a warm but light place (a window-sill is ideal) but at no time should the rays of the sun be allowed to shine directly on the unrooted cuttings. During any period of strong sun, the cuttings should either be moved or protected by a sheet of newspaper or horticultural fleece.

No further action needs to be taken until rooting has been completed. No further watering will be necessary because the moisture contained in the jar cannot escape and will be recycled by transpiration and condensation. After about three weeks, the centres of the young cuttings will take on a brighter, perkier look, which indicates that rooting has commenced. Allow a further week and then begin the process of gently weaning the rooted cuttings from the cloistered atmosphere of their propagator: unscrew the lid for a short period over a couple of days and then finally remove the lid permanently. The tray can then be removed from the sweet jar. From now onwards, the cuttings can be treated as individual young plants: they can be potted on into their own fairly small pots and their training can commence.

ROOTING IN BLOCKS OF OASIS STEP-BY-STEP

Bearing in mind that fuchsia cuttings will root given moisture and warmth it is obvious that any type of medium capable of holding moisture can be used for this purpose. Flower arrangers notice how very often the twigs used to provide foliage start to produce small roots in the blocks of oasis used to support the plant material, which indicates that an oasis can be used to root cuttings. Indeed, it has proved to be a very simple and effective way of ensuring success when rooting fuchsia cuttings, and of course it has the added advantages that it is very easy to work with and does not produce the mess associated with rooting cuttings in compost.

You will need:

❀ A brick of oasis
❀ A sharp hobby knife
❀ A flower stick
❀ Plastic labels and marker pen
❀ Container to accommodate the oasis
  (plastic ice-cream containers are ideal)

1. Remove a slice of oasis about 2in (5cm) thick from the brick of oasis, and soak it in water until it is completely saturated. Score a grid on the top of the oasis so that each cutting will have its own separate compartment (above).

2. Using the sharp knife, take a cutting and insert into the oasis. With soft tip cuttings, it will be necessary to make a small hole in the oasis with the flower stick to prevent damage to the delicate stems, but cuttings will, if cut at an angle, slip very easily into it without other assistance. Label each cutting or group of cuttings and then place the completely planted block of oasis into the container. Add water

ROOTING IN BLOCKS OF OASIS STEP-BY-STEP

to the container so that the oasis is standing in water. The water in the container will ensure that humidity is maintained around the cuttings, so it is unnecessary to cover the cuttings with moisture-retaining plastic. Rooting will take place in two to three weeks (left).

3. When rooting is completed, the cuttings can be transferred, but no attempt must be made to remove the cuttings from the oasis. They can be separated from each other by removing each in its own small core of oasis. Although this involves cutting through young roots no great damage will be caused to the rooted cuttings (below left).

4. Each should now be potted individually in your usual potting compost in a pot sufficiently large to hold the core of oasis easily (below).

5. The oasis core should be completely buried beneath the surface of the compost so that no part of it is showing. Failure to do this will mean that moisture will be leached from the oasis as it dries in the air with strangulation of the root system resulting (below).

Although perfectionists will say that rooting has effectively taken place in water and that the root system is therefore likely to be very brittle, burying the cores of oasis in this way means that there is no delay in the development of the root system and the subsequent development of the plant.

It will be necessary to provide some shading in the confines of a greenhouse.

The cuttings should be prevented from wilting at all costs, being looked at daily and, if necessary, being given a spray with fresh water. Cuttings in coffee jars will not need this attention, as the moisture within the pot is unable to escape. For the best possible success in rooting, you should aim for a temperature of approximately 60°F (15–16°C).

Cuttings that are not grown in propagators should be sprayed regularly to prevent them from wilting.

Within ten to fourteen days indications should appear to tell you that the cuttings are beginning to form their roots. Shortly after the cuttings are removed from the parent plants they will take on a rather dull look, but when rooting commences a healthy, glossy look appears and the cuttings begin to look more sprightly. At this stage the cuttings should be left in their ideal situations for another week so that all the cuttings in the container have the opportunity of forming roots. To prevent any shock to the young plants, it is advisable to wean them away gently from their humid environment. Raise the edge of the propagator top for a short time during the first two days to allow fresh air to pass among the cuttings. Gradually increase the amount of air allowed to the plants until, by the end of the week, the propagator top can be completely removed from its position, and the young plants will be able to survive quite happily.

The cuttings can remain in their containers for a further week before it will be necessary to consider placing them in their individual pots. If the compost in which you rooted your cuttings contained no nutrients (perhaps a 50/50 mixture of peat and perlite), it will be necessary to add some food to the compost by watering with a dilute liquid feed. I would suggest a high nitrogen feed, diluted to a quarter of the normal recommended strength (1 level teaspoon to four gallons (18 litres) of water). If your compost contained some nutrient there will be no need to start feeding until the first potting has taken place.

WHEN TO TAKE CUTTINGS

Cuttings may be taken at any time of the year, provided the correct amount of warmth can be given. If you wish to obtain good-sized plants for flowering in early to late summer, then the earlier the cuttings are rooted the better. Cuttings rooted in late winter/early spring will grow into plants large enough to be placed and flower in 5–6in (13–15cm) pots by mid-summer. Cuttings may be taken (as an insurance policy), in late summer or early autumn, from plants growing in the garden which will be left in that situation. Over-wintering young green tip cuttings inside your house will ensure that, should a severe frost cause the demise of any plant in the open garden, you will have a new, young plant ready to replace it in the spring.

OTHER CUTTINGS

Many growers of the superb plants exhibited on show benches prefer to grow their fuchsias using the 'biennial' method. That is, they will grow their plants to a certain size in the first year and will allow them to flower the following year, having trained them into very bushy plants or standards. Cuttings for this type of growth are usually taken in late spring/early summer when no artificial warmth will be necessary, and the young plants are allowed to develop into bushy shapes by continual 'stopping' of the growing tips. Such plants do not have a winter's rest but are encouraged to stay in green leaf through the winter months, being kept at sufficient temperature to ensure they remain live.

It is possible to take harder wood cuttings of plants in the late autumn, and these can be rooted

'Orient Express' in a mixed border.

by being left in a cold frame throughout the winter. This is not a particularly satisfactory method, but it is the means by which plants can be grown to be used later as hedges.

The secret of success in the rooting of cuttings is to maintain a humid atmosphere around the young cutting so that it does not lose its turgidity by too great a transpiration. If the base of the cutting material is kept moist and the leaves do not flag, then rooting will certainly take place.

CROSSING

When talking about propagation you automatically think of taking cuttings from a plant and encouraging rooting – propagation can really be defined as increasing by natural process, and there are other means by which you can increase the number of your fuchsias. Taking cuttings (removing a piece of a parent plant) will give you, when it is rooted, an exact copy of the original plant – a cutting from 'Border Queen' will become a plant of 'Border Queen'. This means that you are able easily to increase the amount of stock you hold of any one type of plant. However, it does not enable you to produce new types of plants – new cultivars. The taking of a cutting from a plant is known as 'vegetative reproduction', while the way in which new cultivars can be obtained, by the crossing of one cultivar with another, is known as 'sexual reproduction'. The resultant seed obtained from such crossings will produce a new plant which bears the characteristics of each of its parents, and is different from its seed-bearing parent.

New cultivars can be easily obtained, as is shown by the vast number (some ten thousand) which are available today. Unfortunately many of the 'new' cultivars are very similar to those already obtainable, and are no improvement upon them. The work of a hybridizer should always be to improve what is already obtainable, in terms of resistance to disease,

'Cliff's Own', a hybrid resulting from a cross between 'Christine Clements' and 'Cloverdale Pearl'. An excellent plant, especially in the smaller pots.

strength of stem, greater flowering potential, colour, and so on. It is important therefore that any prospective plant breeder should have the strength of character to be selective. A ripe berry from a fuchsia plant may produce scores of seeds, all of which, if given the right conditions, will germinate and grow into flowering plants. Many of these will be inferior plants with many weaknesses, others will be very similar to other cultivars, and very few will show an improvement upon what has gone before. The breeder should, as soon as the type of growth and flower is known, sort out those which are worthy of further consideration, and then dispose of the rest. A really dedicated breeder will save perhaps a dozen from a thousand or more seedlings. Strength of character is certainly necessary.

The methods by which the pollen of one plant is transferred to another plant for fertilization to take place are discussed fully in other publications, and the grower who is anxious to try his hand at hybridizing will need to make a study of the subject in order to formulate a programme of research and improvement. Each hybridizer needs to have an aim and should have a mental picture of the type of plant he or she is attempting to produce.

SEEDS

It is possible to obtain packets of fuchsia seeds which, when grown, will produce new plants. As already stated, plants resulting from the sowing of such seed will be new cultivars and might well be extremely disappointing. Conversely, it is possible that one excellent new cultivar might be found which will be a complete breakthrough from anything that has gone before. One of the problems about buying packets of seed concerns the percentage of germination that you should be prepared to accept. For the best possible results, seeds from the fuchsia should be sown as soon as possible after removal from the berry. There will inevitably be a long delay from harvesting to sowing when seeds are purchased. An ordinary seed sowing compost is suitable, and it is recommended that the seed should not be buried but lightly pressed into the surface of the compost. The compost should be kept moist by watering from below or very gently spraying from above. If a temperature of 65–70°F (18–21°C) can be maintained, germination should occur very quickly. When the seedlings are large enough to handle they should be pricked out into individual small pots and then grown on in the same way as small rooted cuttings. Beware of damping off disease brought about by a lack of ventilation.

TIP
Do not be in a hurry to throw away the compost in which your seedlings were germinated, as it is possible that other seedlings will appear later. It is worth waiting for these, as it is often the case that those seeds which have been slower to germinate produce the nicest plants.

SPORTING

The production and the sowing of seeds is not the only method by which new varieties can be produced. Occasionally, plants produce a shoot which has flowers or leaves of a different colour or shape – this is known as 'sporting'. It is surprising how plants of the same cultivar, in vastly differing parts

'Alice Topliss', a 'Lady Ramsay' sport.

'Cliff's Unique', the first known double flower to be held erect.

'Florence Mary Abbot' is useful in hanging baskets and as a supported bush in the container.

of the country, will in the same season start producing such branches. (Unfortunately, this multi-production of 'sports' usually means that different names are given to the same type of plants by the growers.) The finding of branches which are different from the parent plant is a matter of observation. Growers who are really looking after their plants and handling them daily are far more likely to notice the variation in colour of a flower or leaf. If you find such a 'sport', it will be important for you to secure new plants from the varying branch. To secure the new variety you just need to take cuttings from that branch, and such cuttings will hopefully reproduce the new colouring. You will probably have to grow such new plants for two or three years, to ensure that the new colouring has

'Pink Surprise', a 'Swingtime' sport.

been fixed and that the plant does not revert to the colouring of its parent.

When you produce a new cultivar, whether it is by growing a new seedling or by securing a 'sport', it is advisable to ask the advice of other enthusiastic growers of fuchsias as to the relative merits of your new 'baby'. If the response obtained is favourable, you should grow the new plant to its full potential, in as many differing shapes as possible, and put it forward for public examination on the show bench at a specialist fuchsia show. The judges will be able to advise you on the future prospects of your plants. If you have been extremely lucky and have produced a potential winner, a specialist fuchsia nurseryman will certainly be interested in discussing your plant with you. No fortunes have ever been made in producing new

fuchsias, but there is considerable satisfaction is seeing the name of your introduction appearing among the winners at national shows.

NAMING YOUR FUCHSIA CULTIVAR

The naming of fuchsias is very much a personal matter, but you should bear in mind that names which are already in use should not be given to a new plant. There is an International Registrar based in America for the registration of fuchsia names but there is, unfortunately, no legal requirement that names should be registered. The International Registrar of Fuchsias can be contacted at The American Fuchsia Society, Hall of Flowers, Garden Centre of San Francisco, 9th Avenue and Lincoln Way, San Francisco, California 94122, USA.

CHAPTER 4

Shaping your Plants

When your cuttings are well rooted and beginning to grow you will need to consider for what purpose you intend to use them. If you just leave them now, they will continue to grow straight up the central stem, wandering around rather like a vine, and will soon be out of control. The number of flowers is determined by the number of branches or 'laterals' on the plant, so you need to encourage your fuchsias to produce as many branches as possible (unless you want to grow a standard fuchsia).

'Golden Dawn' requires early stopping to make a good shape.

STOPPING

Generally, people want good bushy plants, but the natural desire of most fuchsias is to grow straight along the central stem. For this reason you need to encourage side shoots to form, in order to prevent that upward growth. When your rooted cutting has produced three or four sets of leaves, you can remove the small growing tip from the centre of the plant. The result of this 'stopping' of the plant is that those young shoots in the leaf axils will receive all the nutrient that would have made its way to the leading growing tip, and each will now start to develop and grow into a new young branch. Where you had one growing tip, if there were three pairs of leaves on the plant when 'stopped', you will now have six – six new branches which will produce for you six times the quantity of flowers. If you allow these six branches to develop until they have each produced two or three pairs of leaves, you can then remove the growing tip from each of them, and this will mean that on each branch four or six new branches should grow. If you multiply this by the six branches you will see that you now have a nice bushy plant, with either twenty-four or thirty-six branches, and you will not have to do any further 'stopping' of your plants.

If you wish, you can continue the process each time the new shoots produce two pairs of leaves, and your plants will become bigger and bushier. However, you must remember that the action of stopping the growth encourages the production of new branches and will delay the production of flower buds. The buds are formed in the very tips of each branch, so the removal of those tips delays flowering until new ones have been grown. As a rough guide, if the flowers from your plant are usually single (four petals only), then there will be a delay of about eight

STOPPING STEP-BY-STEP

Before starting, ensure that the young plants have been well watered and are quite turgid, otherwise the growing tip will not snap off so easily.

1. Remove the growing tip. The smallest piece possible should be removed: with the tip of your finger, gently bend the small tip at right angles to the first pair of leaves and it will snap off very easily without  damaging any of the small shoot buds that may be in the leaf axils. Some growers remove the small tip with scissors or a razor blade, while others resort to finger and thumb nails; each of these methods is dangerous for these small developing shoots.

2. The buds in the axils of the leaves remaining on the plant after this initial stopping will develop into new growth. These new branches should also be stopped in the same way as before.

3. New shoots should grow from the leaf axils on each of the stopped branches. You can continue in this way, stopping new branches to encourage further growth until optimum bushiness has been achieved, after which stopping should cease so that the plant can begin to produce flowers.

The growth of a plant as a result of stopping.

weeks before flowers appear. If your plant produces double flowers (five or more petals in the corolla), an additional two weeks must be allowed before the flowers can be expected.

The earlier in the season you can start your training of the plants, the bigger they can become and the more flowers they will eventually bear. Generally, for the purpose of outdoor displays, just two 'stoppings' will be sufficient to give some excellent plants. Those gardeners growing for show or exhibition purposes will undoubtedly require a greater number of 'breaks'.

If you wish to produce plants suitable for use in baskets (usually plants which have shown a rather lax type of growth, and will cascade down over the edge of the basket), the type of training described above is all that you need. The young plants can be 'stopped' at three pairs of leaves and then 'stopped' for a second time when a further three pairs of leaves have been formed. This will give you nice bushy plants which can be placed around your basket, and will give you an excellent show over a long period of time. Plants for planting out permanently in the garden can also be produced in the same way.

If you wish to grow your cuttings into shapes other than bushes or shrubs, a different method of training will need to be adopted.

'Michelle Wallace', a sport from 'Countess of Aberdeen'.

STANDARDS

I have often heard standard fuchsias called tree fuchsias – a very fair description of them, since what they are is a bush fuchsia growing on a stem. First you have to grow the stem.

The natural desire of the fuchsia is to grow straight along the first stem, with all its strength and vigour being concentrated on that central growing tip. Select a good, strong cutting, preferably one with leaves growing in threes along the stem as opposed to the usual twos, place a flower stick alongside the cutting and gently secure the stem to it with soft twine. This will serve two purposes – it will remind you that this cutting is to be grown on as a standard, and should not therefore have its central tip removed, and also it will encourage the stem to grow straight. Ensure that you secure the stem to the cane loosely as it will thicken as it grows, and you do not want to make an indentation into the stem nor

'Mr W. Rundle' makes an excellent weeping standard.

DEVELOPMENT OF A STANDARD STEP-BY-STEP

A strong, upright-growing young plant is needed for standard training, although some cultivars with slightly more lax growth can be trained to make what is known as a weeping standard. A well-balanced 'standard' fuchsia will have a bushy head which takes up about one third of its total height. The type of standard is determined by its length of clear stem: 6–10in (15–25cm) **Mini Standard**; 10–18in (25–45cm) **Quarter Standard**; 18–30in (45–75cm) **Half Standard**; 30–42in (75–105cm) **Full Standard**.

1. Place a flower stick alongside the cutting and tie in the stem with soft twine. Remove all side shoots from the leaf axils. Do not, however, remove the side leaves.

2. When the stem has reached about 1ft (30cm), allow the top three sets of shoots to develop; when a fourth set develops below the growing tip, the lowest set can be removed. Continue to remove any side shoots that develop below the three top sets and remember to check the rootball at regular intervals, potting on as necessary.

3. When the stem has reached the desired height, pinch out the growing tip. When the top three sets of side shoots have developed two sets of leaves, pinch out their growing tips, which will encourage the head of the standard to bush out. Continue to remove any side shoots that develop below the head. Pot on the standard into its final pot. There is no need to remove the leaves from the stem as these will die off naturally and in due course fall away.

prevent the passage of nutrients up its length. As the plant develops it is possible that young shoots will appear in the leaf axils up the stem. As these will rob the main growing tip of some of its vigour, it is advisable gently to remove these young shoots as they form. This can be done by bending them at right angles to the stem and so snapping them off cleanly. If they are left until they are much bigger, and then removed with a knife, a scar may result – this will be disfiguring when the plant is mature.

The stem will grow upwards at quite a speed and attention should be paid to the pot in which it is growing. At regular intervals the plant should be removed from the pot and the rootball examined. When a good number of roots are showing on the outside of the compost, and before they have time to start encircling the pot, the plant should be re-potted into the next size of pot and given fresh compost. This new compost will encourage fresh root growth and with that extra root growth will come faster top growth. Failure to pot on into larger pots with fresh compost will cause the plant to become 'pot-bound'. Because of the lack of nutrients available to the roots (even if copious supplies of liquid fertilizer are being fed into the pot), the plant will feel threatened. Its reaction will be to produce its flowers, so that seed will be set and the species continued. When the upward-growing standard feels threatened, the flower buds will be formed and upward growth will cease. This is not what you want, so you must

do all you can to ensure the continued vegetative growth of your plant. Regular re-potting will provide the additional nutrients and the root space for continued growth, both below and above the surface of the compost.

It is possible that by the time the plant has reached the height you require (and this can be anything up to about 4ft (120cm)), your plant will have been moved from a 2in (5cm) to a 7in (17.5cm) pot, in 1in (2.5cm) stages.

When the 'whip' (the name for a cutting being grown as a standard) has grown to about 12in (30cm) in height, you can leave the top three sets of shoots in the leaf axils as they develop. As a further set develops at the top of the plant, the lower

POTTING ON A GROWING STANDARD

The mould-forming method of potting on, as described in chapter 2, can usefully be employed here since the same principles apply.

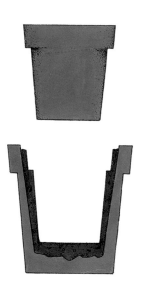

Using a pot of the same size as a 'former'.

Removing the growing plant from its pot.

Replanting in a slightly larger pot.

you have enough patience you can, when two pairs of leaves have grown on each of your branches, remove the growing tips to quadruple the number of branches again.

The eventual height your standard reaches will depend upon your own wishes. However, if at some future date you are so pleased with your standard fuchsia that you would like to enter it in a show, you will need to know the measurements required by the show schedule. A miniature standard is one growing in a 5in (13cm) pot, with a clear stem not in excess of 10in (25cm) – a clear stem is measured from the level of the compost to the first branch. A quarter standard is one on which the stem is no less than 10in (25cm), nor more than 18in (45cm). A

'Celia Smedley', an extremely versatile, floriferous cultivar that is easy to train.

set can be removed, so that you always have three sets of shoots available to form a head in case anything should happen to the growing tip.

When the whip reaches the height you require, having three sets of shoots in the top three sets of leaf axils, the process of forming the bush on the top of your stem can commence. Remove the growing tip. This will now encourage all the strength and vigour of the plant to go into those three sets of shoots which you have left on the plant. They will grow, and when they have each formed two sets of leaves, their growing tips can be removed. Your six (or nine) branches in the head can now be multiplied by four. This could be sufficient in the first season, and you can then allow each of these branches to develop and produce their flowers. If

As its name suggests, 'Howlett's Hardy' makes a good border subject. It has unusually large blooms for a hardy cultivar.

NOTE

Even if the cultivar you have used to grow your standard is considered a 'hardy' variety, it should not be left in the garden over winter, as the very first severe frost will kill the stem. As it takes at least six months to grow this stem it would be a pity to lose it. Standards do need extra protection during the winter (*see* Chapter 6).

---

half standard has a clear stem of between 18in (45cm) and 30in (75cm). A full standard commences at 30in (75cm), and does not exceed 42in (105cm). Usually in the case of the quarter, half and full standards, the size of the pot is irrelevant, although it ought to be in proportion to the plant.

Standard fuchsias are ideal subjects for planting out in the garden during the summer as 'dot' plants. They give that very important extra height

'Fenman' makes an excellent standard for the border.

'Radings Karin' is a good subject for shaping with wire and training as a fan, espalier or a miniature standard.

to any flower bed, and are always a very good focus and talking point.

These paragraphs cover only the simplest forms of training, and there are others which I would suggest are worth trying when you have gained greater expertise in the growing of these plants. It is possible to grow fuchsias as pillars, pyramids, fans and espaliers, but it will be important to have sufficient space available for the over-wintering and growing of these larger specimens. They are extremely time-consuming and, as they can be growing and flowering for you over a period of eight or more years, they can become very much a part of the family and somewhat of a liability when holidays, and so on, are being planned! At the other end of the spectrum it is also possible to train fuchsias in miniature as bonsai trees.

METHODS OF TRAINING FOR SPECIFIC SHAPES

As with the training of standards, it is important to select a strong, upright-growing cultivar for training into the following shapes and to support the plant with a flower stick.

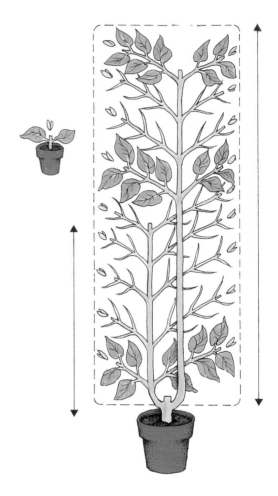

Pyramid Shape
Remove the growing tip at three sets of leaves and select the stronger of the two shoots as leader. Allow the side shoots to develop. When a further three sets of leaves have formed on the 'leader' remove the growing tip and select the shoot on the opposite side to the first 'leader' to continue as the new 'leader'. Continue to allow the side shoots to develop but remove their growing tips, when appropriate, to encourage bushiness and upward growth.

Pillar Formation
At two sets of leaves remove the growing tip. Encourage both resultant shoots to grow upwards. Allow the side shoots to develop on one but remove them from the other. When approximately half of the intended height of the structure has been achieved remove the growing tip of the one whose side shoots have been growing and encourage the strong upward growth of the other – now leaving in its side shoots. The side shoots also must be stopped to encourage bushiness and an evenness of growth to the complete height.

METHODS OF TRAINING FOR SPECIFIC SHAPES

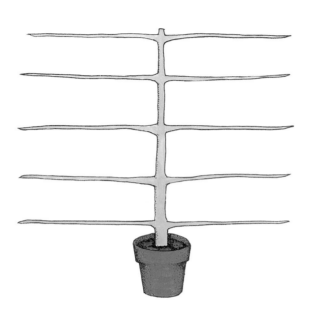

Espalier
Allow the side shoots, on a strong upright growing plant, to develop removing the alternate sets of shoots so that all are growing as a flat structure. A frame work needs to be assembled so that the laterals are trained in the horizontal position. When sufficient width has been achieved the shoots are 'stopped' to encourage growths from the leaf axils along the stems. Remove those which create too much depth to the structure and encourage those which 'fill in' the frame work.

Fan Shape
Remove the growing tip when four sets of leaves have formed on a strong upright growing plant. Remove the alternate resulting shoots so that the new branches will form the fan shape. Tie the young branches onto a fan shaped structure and encourage the side shoots to grow but removing those which create too much depth. Remove the growing tips of each of the main branches, selecting one of the resulting tip shoots to act as a new 'leader'. Regular tying in of the new growths will be necessary to achieve a fan covered with foliage and flowers.

CHAPTER 5

Displaying Fuchsias

FUCHSIAS IN THE GARDEN

Fuchsias will combine with practically any other type of flower to make an extremely good show in the garden. There are really two ways in which one can approach the use of fuchsias in the garden: as half-hardy annuals used as temporary bedding subjects, or as permanent bedding plants. (They can also be used as hedging, but really the permanent bedding and hedging can be treated as one.)

Bearing in mind that fuchsias are frost-shy plants, the initial planting of either temporary or permanent bedding schemes should be left until all risk of frost has passed – usually not until early summer. It should also be borne in mind that when planting in a permanent border great care needs to be taken over the preparation of the site, as the plants, once established, will remain in the same position for many years. The ground will need to be well dug, and a quantity of fertilizer should be added for a good food supply for the foraging roots. It is beneficial to dig in quantities of peat so that the earth surrounding the plants remains moist.

As with all bedding schemes, far greater impact is made on the eye if a group of plants of the same cultivar are planted together, perhaps in groups of three or five. Care should also be taken to ensure that the plants used will grow to a reasonable height, with those expected to reach the greatest height at the back of the border. On a temporary basis, quarter, half or full standards are extremely useful to give that all-important height. Under no circumstances should plants trained as standards be allowed to remain in the garden when frosts threaten. The first severe frost will kill off the stem and all the time and trouble taken to grow it will have been wasted.

Simple plan for the layout of a fuchsia bed, with the low-growing 'Thumb' family in the front and standards in the centre.

The hardy border.

Strong, upright-growing plants should be chosen, preferably those which hold their flowers in the semi-horizontal or upright positions. For temporary use it is not necessary to confine yourself to those plants which are considered to be hardy (that is, capable of remaining in the same position throughout the winter and sending up fresh young shoots the following spring). You can therefore choose any from the long lists of plants now available, when choosing your colour scheme it might be as well to consider the colouring of the leaves. Plants of the *triphylla* type with their dark green leaves and purple underleaf are extremely attractive, even while you are awaiting the arrival of the flowers. There are other variegated and yellow-leaved varieties which are equally useful.

When planting your border you should space your plants, which hopefully will be growing in 3½in (9cm) or 5in (13cm) pots, at a distance of 15–18in (37.5–45cm) apart. For those which will be remaining in the site permanently, the method of planting will make a considerable difference to their hardiness. After the first severe frosts in the autumn, the plants will be denuded of leaves and the protection of the rootball will be your primary consideration. You will need to give each rootball some protection or insulation from deep frosts, as it is from the rootball that you hope new shoots will grow in the following spring. To give this extra protection from severe frosts it is advisable to plant your fuchsias deeper than is normally recommended for other flowering shrubs. The usual recommendation is to plant at the same level in the ground as the surface of the compost in the pot. However, although this will give some protection, the top of the rootball will be very near the surface of the soil. You should really aim to get that rootball about 2in (5cm) lower than the soil surface and

PROTECTING THE HARDY BORDER PLANT

1. In the spring, fresh new growth will appear from below the surface of the soil and beneath the protection offered by the old branches (above left).

2. When the fresh growth is quite strong...(above)

3. ...you can cut away the old branches to make room for the new flowering branches (left).

4. Once the debris has been cleared away from the base of the plant, a mulch of mushroom compost, well-rotted compost or any other type of mulching will help to maintain moistness around the young emerging shoots. A light sprinkling, raked into the surface, of a general purpose fertilizer will be beneficial (opposite top).

5. In early spring, growth of the young shoots will be rapid. The delightful young yellow foliage of *F.* 'Genii' will give colour to the border before the plant starts to produce its flowers (opposite).

one of the easiest ways of doing this, without immediately covering some of the lower branches and leaves with soil, is to prepare a saucer-shaped indentation in the ground, about 2in (5cm) deep in the centre, for each plant. At the centre of each saucer the fuchsia can be planted so that its compost level is the same as the lower level of the soil. During the course of the summer, with the water-

Do not be tempted to remove the branches from your permanent bedding plants when the first frosts have removed the leaves. Leave them on the plants until the spring, as they will give added protection from the severe frosts and will also indicate the position of each plant. In the spring, when fresh growth is being produced from below the surface of the soil, you can cut away the old branches to make room for the new flowering branches that will grow.

Although your fuchsias have been planted in a well-cultivated piece of ground, it is unwise to assume that they can now be left to fend for themselves. They will need the same sort of treatment that you give to plants growing in pots. Watering will need to be carried out, especially at the beginning of the season as the plants become established, and also in those long, dry, sunny spells we all dream about. Regular feeding will pay dividends as it will encourage fresh young growth and a multitude of flowers. Keep an eye open also for pests and diseases. In the open the capsid bug is a bit of a problem, as it bites the succulent young tip of the shoots, causing loss of flowering. A regular spraying with a systemic insecticide will keep your plants clear. White fly is less of a problem in the open, but it is something that does need to be watched for.

As the flowering season draws to a close you may become worried about the possibility of your plants not surviving the winter. If so, there is nothing to stop you from lifting some of the plants, cleaning them and storing them in pots or boxes in a frost-free place. However, it is better to leave your plants in the garden, giving them a little extra protection with peat, bracken or other insulating material. Also, you could take some pre-winter cuttings in case of disaster. You may have noticed in the heavy misty mornings of autumn that the fuchsias seem to take on a new lease of life. Fresh, young, green growth appears on the ends of most branches as the plants experience the type of humid, moist, conditions which they enjoy so much in their native habitat. Small pieces of these new shoots can be removed from the plants as green tip cuttings. If placed in a propagator they will root quite readily with no additional warmth, and can be nurtured through the winter with very little difficulty. At this stage of the season there is no rush for root formation, so a simple unheated propagator in a cool

ing and cultivating around the plants, the saucer shape will be filled in and the rootball will be a couple of inches lower than the normal soil level. This means important extra insulation.

Planting in the garden using a saucer-shaped indentation so that the plant is inserted at the correct level.

'Tinkerbell' is a hardy cultivar with upright and yet dainty, arching growth. It does well in the front of the border and is also suited to the rockery.

RECOMMENDED CULTIVARS FOR THE GARDEN

Alice Hoffman, Brutus, Charming, Display, Dorothy, Empress of Prussia, Garden News, Genii, Herald, Lady Thumb, Margaret, Margaret Brown, Pixie, Rufus (the Red), Snowcap, Son of Thumb, Tennessee Waltz, and Tom Thumb.

This is a very brief list of suitable cultivars for permanently bedding outside, and a glance through any nurseryman's catalogue will give names of many others. Within these catalogues you will often see the codes 'H1', 'H2', and 'H3'. These codes can be defined as follows:

H1 requires a greenhouse heated to a minimum of 40°F (4 to 5°C)
H2 requires cool greenhouse – half-hardy
H3 denotes that the plant is considered hardy

---

place will be ideal. Rooting could take up to four weeks in such conditions, and the resultant plants can be allowed to remain within the propagators in a frost-free place, growing slowly as the winter months progress. If the rooted cuttings start to outgrow their container, perhaps in late autumn or early winter, then the process can be repeated, the tips of each rooted cutting being used to make fresh soft green tip cutting material. By the time the fresh young cuttings have rooted and are growing well, spring will be just around the corner and a supply of bedding plants will be ready, just in case your outdoor plants have succumbed to the wintry weather.

FUCHSIAS ON THE PATIO

There is no better way to show off your fuchsias than by growing them out of doors and it does not really matter whether you have a large garden or just a small area – the fuchsia will enhance your surroundings and will be a focal point around which other plants can grow. On the patio, you will be growing your plants in what might be considered to

be unnatural conditions (within confined root spaces). However, growing plants in tubs or baskets is no different from growing plants in pots in the greenhouse, and as such is quite possible.

There are various containers that are available for use, but your immediate instinct might be to raise the plants away from the ground, where they can be viewed from their best possible angle. Looking up into the pendulous flowers is the way to admire their shape and form. Suspending plants growing in hanging baskets or pots is therefore most important, and baskets can be successfully fixed to the walls so that flowers can cascade down. If there is insufficient room for full-sized baskets it might well be possible to suspend hang-

The semi-double 'Margaret', a hardy cultivar that reaches a height and spread of 4ft (120cm), making it ideal for the back of the border.

There is no reason why fuchsias cannot be grown in a mixed container to make an eye-catching display (below).

Hardy, bush-grown fuchsias in a permanent position in the garden border.

ing pots. At ground level, troughs of various shapes and sizes can be used, as can large ornamental urns. Window-sills make ideal resting places for narrow troughs where plants can be appreciated from both inside and outside the house. You do not need to confine yourself to the type of container that can be purchased, however. there is a great deal of satisfaction in being able to manufacture suitable containers yourself, or recycling objects made for another purpose.

Although some enthusiasts of the fuchsia would prefer to see their favourite plants growing in isolation, I feel that fuchsias grown in coordination with other types of annuals, hardy or half-hardy, will produce a beautiful display.

It is important when considering these outdoor displays to remember that you are dealing with frost-tender plants, and that it would be unwise to place them in their final flowering positions until all risks of frost have passed – not until early summer. Even after that time, you should keep an eye on the weather forecast and, should a frost warning be given, take the necessary and simple protective actions.

Any type of fuchsia will be suitable for use in the patio garden. Plants for the hanging pots and baskets need to be of the laxer pendulous type, but upright growers of all shapes and hues will be suitable for ground containers.

Baskets

It is always a good idea for a basket of fuchsias to contain a number of plants of the same cultivar. If a variety of cultivars is used you will find that their rate of growth and time of flowering will vary. A basket completely covered with foliage and flowers is a marvellous sight, and it should look the same, whichever angle it is viewed from. The number of plants you require for each basket will depend upon its diameter – a basket with a diameter of 12in (30cm) will need four plants of a strong growing cultivar (three around the edge and one in the centre); a 15in (37.5cm) basket will need five. Most basket varieties are strong vigorous growers but some, especially those with smaller leaves and small flowers, will require additional plants, so that the basket is a complete ball of flower.

Although the basket will not be placed in its final position (from a bracket attached to the house, or on a pedestal) until early summer, it is advisable to make arrangements for the basket to be planted with well-grown plants and to be kept growing strongly in a warm environment ahead of this date. The best basket plants will be those grown from cuttings taken very early in the year, or even during the previous autumn. Preferably they will be growing in 3½in (9cm) pots and will have good, well-branched growth. The wire hemispherical-shaped

'Rosy Frills', a good basket subject with large vivid blooms.

'Cream Puff', an ideal subject for the hanging container.

baskets are perhaps the most popular, and should be planted as follows.

The shape (rounded bottom) of the basket will make it difficult to keep the container still during the planting operation – try placing the basket in a large flower pot, tub or bucket. The first requirement will be some substance to prevent the compost from falling through the gaps in the wire. Many growers use moss for this purpose, but I prefer to use a sheet of plastic, preferably black, cut to size. Drainage holes need to be made in this plastic sheet so that excess water can escape. A pre-formed liner available for the purpose is a very convenient alternative. The compost should be a peat-based one, as the weight of a basket filled with a loam-based compost is too great.

Baskets are open to the drying elements of the wind and the sun, and will therefore need watering daily – perhaps even twice a day in the height of the

PLANTING A BASKET STEP-BY-STEP

You will need:

❀ A wire basket
❀ A bucket or similar container that will support the basket during the planting process
❀ A preformed basket liner, or plastic sheet with drainage holes cut to size
❀ Peat-based compost
❀ Empty pots of the same size as those from which the plants are to be transferred, one to represent each plant in the basket
❀ Watering can with a fine rose

1. Rest the basket on the bucket and then place the liner in the basket. Add three or four handfuls of just-moist compost to give you a layer of about 2in (5cm) in the base of the basket. The mould-forming method of potting on, as described in Chapter 2, can once again be used here: arrange the empty pots on the compost. (Some growers recommend that the outer pots are placed at a slight angle to encourage the foliage to trail over the edge of the basket, but this is not necessary.)

2. Once you are satisfied that the pots represent the desired final positions of the plants, pour compost into and around them until both they and the basket are full. The rims of the pots should be just visible and the compost surrounding them settled by bouncing the basket on its base. Remove the pot nearest the centre of the basket to leave a pot-shaped indentation in the compost. Remove one plant from its pot by inverting it and place it in the indentation.

summer. Care must therefore be taken to ensure that they are easily accessible and that a supply of water is to hand. As flowers are produced and then die, it is important to ensure that seed pods are removed in order to maintain a constant supply of flowers throughout the season – once the plant's task of producing seeds has been performed, flowering will slow down and perhaps even stop. It will also be necessary to feed the plants during the sea-

son to maintain their vigour – high nitrogen feed in the early part of the season, balanced feed during the summer months and a high potash feed later. Try to get into a habit of feeding your plants on a regular basis so that there is no possibility of this task being forgotten. Whilst feeding or watering, keep a wary eye open for any pests that may be around. Plants growing out of doors seem to suffer far less than their indoor compatriots, but never-

PLANTING A BASKET STEP-BY-STEP

3. Repeat the process for each of the other plants, dealing with them one at a time. (This is especially important when planting a basket because the 'walls' of the indentations may collapse if you try to remove all the pots at once.)

4. When the last plant is in position, the whole basket can be given a good watering to settle the compost further and then – if it has been made up prior to the recommended date for planting outside – transferred to the protection of the greenhouse where the plants can grow and become fully established. When the plants have formed three sets of leaves, pinch out the growing tips and encourage the outer plants to grow outwards and cascade over the edge of the container (below left).

5. In early summer, the basket can be moved to its final position outside, either placed on a pedestal or hung from a wall bracket. The advantage of planting it well in advance will now be apparent in that the well-established plants will afford you an immediately attractive, bushy display, which will soon be followed by the flowers (below).

theless they are very popular with both greenfly and white fly. A regular spraying programme to prevent the build-up of any of these pests is advisable.

Half baskets, or 'wall baskets' as they are sometimes called, are dealt with in a similar way. A bas-ket with a width of 12in (30cm) should hold four plants, three around the front edge and one central. Perhaps the easiest way to keep these baskets still while working on them is to place two back to back within a large pot, tub or bucket. Fixing these

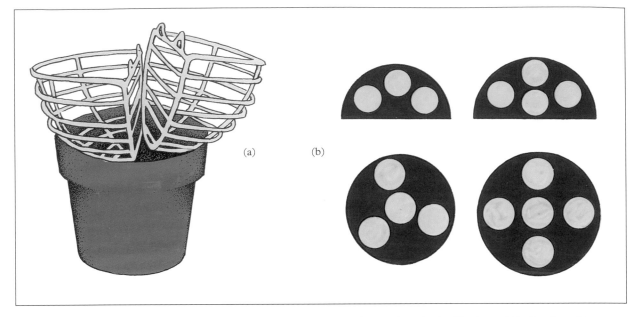

(a) Supporting wire half baskets while planting. (b) Positions for planting in half and full baskets.

'Orange Blossom', with its trailing growth and distinctive flowers with folded petals, makes an attractive subject for the basket.

baskets to the wall is a fairly easy task, but you must make sure that the rear of the basket is parallel to the wall, so that the compost is not tipping forward.

It is not at all necessary to stick to the conventional shapes for your baskets. Let your imagination wander and I am sure you will see the possibilities of making baskets of your own shape and design with all types of materials. Square wooden baskets made with slats of cedar wood, for example, look particularly attractive.

If you do not wish to confine your baskets to fuchsias there are many other plants which will be complemented by and are complementary to them. The blue of the lobelia and the white of the allysum, together with begonias (both *pendulous* and *semperflorum*), pelargoniums, *impatiens* ('Busy Lizzie'), and various foliage plants are all useful in this respect.

Other Containers

Troughs of fuchsias and other plants free-standing on the patio can be very effective, and it is possible to use plants trained in upright forms, standards, pyramids, and so on, to give added height.

A tender, triphylla-*type fuchsia grown with other plants to make a stunning summer display on the patio.*

Specimen plants such as these, with other plants being used as compost coverers, are very useful. A great deal of imagination can be used to find the right type of containers, and any ideas you have to produce some novel container will not be wasted. For example, a wooden wheelbarrow overflowing with flowers, or an old farm cart wheel used to support small half baskets, can be very effective.

So, you can use fuchsias wherever you want, or wherever you need to. If there is a hole in the patio paving put in a fuchsia, if you have a manhole to hide, cover it with a tub of fuchsias, and have fuchsias from the ground level right the way up to the eaves.

RECOMMENDED CULTIVARS FOR THE PATIO

The following is a short list of cultivars recommended for growing in pots and tubs on the patio. They will need to be taken inside during the winter for protection. This is a personal choice and it should be realized that any fuchsias can be used in this way – the variety is endless.

Annabel, Ann H. Tripp, Autumnale, Ballet Girl, Billy Green, Bon Accorde, Border Queen, Cambridge Louie, Celia Smedley, Cloverdale Pearl, Dark Eyes, Dollar Princess, Estelle Marie, Foxtrot, Joan Smith, Joy Patmore, King's Ransom, Marilyn Olsen, Margaret Pilkington, Mipam, Mrs Lovell Swisher, Pacquesa, Perry Park, Royal Velvet, Taddle, and Thalia.

The following is a short list of cultivars which have a lax type of growth and are therefore suitable for use in hanging baskets or wall baskets.

Annabel, Auntie Jinks, Cascade, Golden Marinka, Harry Gray, La Campanella, Marinka, Pink Galore, Pink Marshmallow, President Margaret Slater, President Stanley J. Wilson, and Swingtime.

GROWING PLANTS INDOORS

Many people are introduced to the pleasure of growing fuchsias as a result of having been given a plant in full flower, or there might even have been the temptation to purchase a flowering plant from a shop or at a flower show. Unfortunately, disappointment often follows when these plants arrive home, as the flowers start to fade and the new buds which had given so much hope for the future fall from the plant. You need to realize that fuchsias are not really house plants – they do not appreciate the dry conditions which we favour in our homes. In their natural environment on the wooded foothills of the mountains in South America, they have a constant humidity surrounding them. If you can emulate these conditions, which is what you are trying to do in the greenhouse where higher humidity is welcome, your plants will thrive. So, should fuchsias be taken into the home, and is it possible to grow them under these conditions?

Plants growing indoors on a tray containing gravel.

'Aurora Superba', a beautiful cultivar that can be a temperamental grower and requires a lot of warmth to thrive.

The answer can be 'yes' on both counts. However, having a fuchsia indoors will be a temporary pleasure, as it is much better to bring in a full flowering plant, enjoy its beauty for a short period, and then return it to recuperate in a more appropriate environment. To make its temporary visit less traumatic you can try to give it a certain amount of humidity through its branches, and in this respect you cannot do much better than to follow the example of the growers of Africa Violets (*Saintpaulia*). An earthenware saucer or tray, somewhat larger than the base of the flower pot containing your plant, should be filled with gravel or pebbles. Water is added, so that the pot is standing upon moist pebbles, without the base actually being in contact with water. Standing the flower pot in a saucer of water will cause considerable damage and perhaps death to the root system, but the evaporation of the water from the pebble-filled saucer will give the necessary humidity through the branches of the plant, and it will be much happier for it. The same result could be achieved by spraying the leaves of the plant on a daily basis (although this can be damaging to the surrounding furniture if great care is not taken).

The loss of leaves and new flower buds from your plant bought in full flower is caused by a drastic change of environment, with the plant being taken from the perfect growing conditions of a greenhouse into the dry atmosphere of the home. If a plant has been grown within the drier atmosphere of the home from a very early stage, there is no reason why it should not develop fully and flower to perfection. Many people have success in maintaining small collections of fuchsias under these conditions.

For success indoors, it will be necessary to start at the very early stage in the development of the plant, the cutting stage. It is possible to root cuttings on the window-sill and these, with careful attention to their watering, potting, feeding and turning, can develop into good-sized plants. The window-sill of a bathroom would be an ideal situation, with the frosting of the glass cutting out the strong hot glare of the sun, and the atmosphere remaining moist.

'Flyaway' whose large blooms are freely produced on an upright-growing bush.

Careful attention needs to be paid to the amount of light available to the plants. Each plant should be turned a quarter turn each day, so that all sides receive the same amount of light, and elongation of the branches on one side only will not occur. The natural desire of plants is always to grow towards the light.

Regular inspection for watering will be needed and, as all plants will undoubtedly be standing in a plant saucer, it might be advisable to water by pouring into the saucer. If you pour water into the top of the pot it is easy to be over-generous, and make the saucer overflow when the water has drained through the compost. Plants should be allowed to stand in the water in the saucer for approximately fifteen minutes, giving them time to soak up all they need, and surplus water should then be poured away. If the compost in the pot has been allowed to dry out completely, difficulty will be experienced in encouraging the compost to 'take up' the water in the saucer – remember, a damp cloth will soak up much more water than a dry cloth. To overcome this difficulty it is advisable to immerse the pot completely in a bucket or bowl of water until all air bubbles cease to rise. It is to be hoped that by regular attention to the watering such a situation will not arise.

On a regular basis, perhaps once a week, the plants should be either placed in the bath or taken outside and given a thorough spraying over the foliage. This will help to free the pores of the leaves from dust and will add to the humidity around the plant. At the same time the tips of each plant should be carefully examined for any pets. Indoors greenfly seem to appear from nowhere and regular treatment will keep this sap-sucking insect at bay. Whitefly can also be a problem which can only be resolved by regular attention. Any good insecticide spray can be used for this purpose, and there are some special formulations for indoor plants. Read the label carefully to ensure that it is not unsafe to use inside or on fuchsias.

As the roots of the plants fill their pots they should be re-potted into the next size of pot. Always aim to move your plants into a pot no more than 1in (2.5cm) larger than the previous one. Your favourite peat-based compost will be ideal for this purpose, to give your plants fresh material into which the roots can work. When the pot becomes full of roots and nutrients become scarce, the plant will feel threatened and flower buds will be formed so that seeds can be set to continue the life of the species. While the potting-on process is taking place there will be no need to be feeding your plants as the new compost will provide all the extra nutrients required. However when your plants have reached their final size of pot (in the first season of any plant a 5in (13cm) pot is sufficient), a feeding programme needs to be started.

The feeding will follow the same pattern as that recommended for greenhouse plants – a high nitrogen feed in the spring and early summer, a good balanced feed during the summer months, and a high potash feed later in the summer when the plants start to show their flowering buds. The recommended strength of feeding is always shown on the packet or bottle, and should never be exceeded. However, a greater dilution of feed used at each watering will have beneficial effects – try a quarter strength feeding at each watering.

RECOMMENDED CULTIVARS FOR INDOOR GROWING

Bambini, Chang, Dusky Beauty, Frank Saunders, Lady Patricia Mountbatten, Marilyn Olsen, Minirose, Nellie Nuttall, Other Fellow, Saturnus, String of Pearls, Tom West, and Waveney Gem.

Any fuchsia should be suitable for growing under these conditions but it might be advisable to concentrate upon those which have short compact growth and smaller flowers. The larger, more flamboyant flowers tend to be rather straggly in their growth and would become unmanageable within the confines of the home. When visiting shows or displays of fuchsias it might be as well to make a note of those cultivars which have the dwarfer growing habit and obtain these.

The floriferous 'Lady Ramsay', ideal for the show bench.

CHAPTER 6

The Seasons of the Year

It is a job to know when the 'fuchsia year' actually starts and finishes – if it ever does this is. Each season seems to merge with the one that follows. Perhaps nature has not been informed that we like our year to be broken down into manageable compartments. For convenience, I have divided our year into four seasons, all of which have their own particular charm, pleasures and anxieties. Also for convenience I am starting my fuchsia year with the season of new life, spring, although the calendar informs me that I will be part way through its year before that season arrives.

It is fully appreciated that in varying parts of the world the seasons arrive at differing times – I can generalize and hope that the comments that follow within 'the seasons' will be of assistance to all.

SPRING

Examining Overwintered Plants

I always find that early spring is a very exciting time of the year, when it is possible to allow the mind to

CHECKLIST OF MATERIALS FOR THE GROWING SEASON

Spring is a very busy time for most gardeners, and fuchsia growers are no different. Since much has to be done, it makes sense to prepare yourself in advance and, towards the end of the winter, ensure that you have the equipment and materials that you will need for the new season.

❀ Compost. Ensure that you have adequate supplies or the ingredients for making your own.

❀ Pots and propagation modules. Check that you have sufficient numbers of the various sizes that you will need for potting on or potting back your plants, or for rooting cuttings. If you are recycling last year's pots, clean and disinfect them thoroughly.

❀ Propagators. Ensure that they are clean and ready to receive new cuttings, and that you have sufficient numbers for the amount of cuttings that you will take. If you intend to take more cuttings than can comfortably be accommodated in your propagators, collect together sweet jars, coffee jars and other similar containers that can be pressed into service.

❀ Labels and marking pens. An adequate supply of these might seem a minor consideration, but it is extremely frustrating suddenly to find that you haven't sufficient labels to identify new cuttings.

❀ Canes. Flower sticks of 18in (46cm) and 30in (76cm) will be sufficient for most purposes, although

longer ones will be required for work with standards.

❀ Insecticides, fungicides and fertilizers. Check that any such chemicals or preparations that you retain from last year are still usable and that you have adequate supply. Dispose of any whose age is doubtful.

❀ Sharp knives, pruning secateurs. Check that these are clean and sharp ready for taking cuttings and pruning back plants that you have kept in storage for the winter.

❀ Hanging baskets and containers. Check that you have all the items necessary for making up baskets and containers for the patio, and that brackets from which you will suspend containers later in the season are secure.

❀ Watering equipment. Spray bottles and watering cans should be clean and ready for use. Do not forget to ensure you have a fine rose for watering in cuttings and newly potted plants.

❀ Shading materials. Supplies of horticultural fleece or newspaper will be necessary to shade plants and young cuttings from the sun, which can be surprisingly fierce even, on occasion, in spring. You will also need to decide how you will protect the greenhouse from the sun: ensure that you have sufficient green netting or emulsion paint, or a proprietary paint product manufactured for the purpose.

PRUNING FOR NEW GROWTH AND POTTING BACK

You will need:

❀ A sharp pair of secateurs
❀ A flower stick
❀ A bucket of water
❀ A pot smaller than the one in which the plant is currently growing

❀ Fresh compost of the type you usually favour for repotting
❀ Watering can with a fine rose
❀ Horticultural fleece or newspaper for shading
❀ Spray bottle containing pure, tepid water

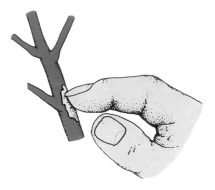

1. Remove the plant from its winter quarters and examine the branches carefully. Provided that the plant has been over-wintered in a frost-free position and that the root system was kept in a just-moist condition, there is no reason why there should not be life in the dead-looking branches. A simple test is to scrape the bark of each branch with a finger nail: if greenness and sap is apparent just below the surface, the branch is alive; if, however, you find dry, brown wood, the branch is probably dead.

2. Using a sharp pair of secateurs, cut back each branch, so that there are just two leaf nodes on each branch.

3. Remove the plant from the pot and tease away all the old compost with the flower stick, being careful not to damage any young white roots that may be showing (another sign that the plant has survived over-wintering). In more stubborn cases, you might find it easier to submerge the rootball in a bucket of water, swilling it around to dislodge the old compost. Examine the old compost for vine weevil larvae. Any present can be dispatched with some satisfaction. However, their presence means that extra vigilance will be required during the growing season to ensure that a further supply of eggs are not laid by any adult weevils that mature from any larvae that you may miss at this stage.

vine weevil larva

PRUNING FOR NEW GROWTH AND POTTING BACK

4. Once the old compost has been removed, it is possible to examine the root system. Using the secateurs, remove any old gnarled roots which have coiled around the pot. You can be fairly ruthless with this activity but do try to maintain an even shape consisting of the young white roots.

5. The plant is now ready to be repotted. Having been pruned the rootball will take up less space and will therefore require a smaller pot, hence the term 'potting back'. For example, it should be possible to pot a plant from a 5 or 6in (12.5 or 15cm) pot into a 3½in (9cm) one. However, the new smaller pot should accommodate the roots comfortably. Place a small quantity of fresh compost in the base of the new pot. Hold the plant in position centrally with one hand, and with the other trickle more fresh compost around the roots. Tap the base of the pot on the bench every now and again to encourage the compost to get in between the roots. Continue this process, supporting the plant at all times, until the pot is full. Give the pot a final tap on the bench to settle the compost. It is not necessary to firm the compost with the fingers. Watering the plant with the fine rose on the watering can, will finally settle the compost. This watering should suffice for the next two or three weeks.

6. Place the newly potted plant in the warmest spot in your greenhouse, or on a window-sill, taking care to shade the plant from hot sun. Inspect the plant daily and spray the young pruned branches with the pure tepid water to soften the top surface of the branches. This will encourage the young dormant shoots in the leaf axils to grow; if you can do this two or three times a day the plant will undoubtedly benefit. This is the only watering that the plant will require, as the excess from the branches falling on to the compost will keep it in the desired just-moist condition.

'Red Spider', a vigorous trailer which needs early stopping to encourage a good shape.

wander ahead and to imagine the beauty of the anticipated flowers. And yet, when the plants kept over the winter are examined, there is sometimes a feeling of depression as one surveys the apparently dead structure. One test is to gently scrape the bark of each branch with a finger nail – if just beneath the surface greenness and sap is seen, the branch is alive. If, however, you find brown dry wood then the probability is that the branch is dead.

To bring the plants back to life all we need to do is to spray the top growths with tepid water on a daily or twice daily basis and keep the plants in a temperature of about 50°F (10°C). There will be no need to water the compost as the excess water from the overhead spraying will maintain a moistness which will be quite adequate. Within two to three weeks of this regular spraying treatment it should be possible to see lovely pink buds appearing along the stems where the leaf axils once grew.

At this stage, when you are aware that your plant is alive and growing, the examination of the root system and the removal of the old compost can be carried out. All the old compost can be carefully teased away ensuring that as little damage as possible is done to the fresh young white roots that are beginning to appear. The old compost should be looked at carefully to see if there are any vine weevil larvae present. If there are they can be dispatched with some satisfaction. The presence of vine weevil larvae will mean that we have to be extra vigilant during the growing season to ensure that a further supply of eggs are not laid by any adult weevils that mature from larvae that we miss.

Repotting overwintered plants, following judicious pruning of old and gnarled roots from the rootball, can be into a pot smaller than that within which it was originally growing. Fresh compost, with its supply of new nutrients, will ensure rapid growth.

'Tom Redfern', whose growth is naturally upright and bushy.

'Greenpeace', a vigorous, rampant grower which needs regular stopping to contain its shape.

Examining Autumn Cuttings

Young plants which have been grown from cuttings taken in the autumn will have been growing steadily throughout the winter provided a temperature around 40°F (4–5°C) has been maintained. It is hoped that as the temperature has been kept at a moderate level the plants will be growing sturdily. If excessive warmth has been given, the growth, as a result of the lack of intensity in the light, will have been rather thin and spindly.

Examine each plant carefully, removing the growing tips if greater bushiness is required or tying in the upright stem if a standard fuchsia is being trained. Any leaves that are yellowing should be removed and a watch should be made for the first signs of aphids, greenfly or whitefly, which also enjoy our overwintering conditions.

Examine the root systems and if the pots are full of roots give extra sustenance to the plants by potting on into larger-sized pots. The usual recommendation is to place the plant in a pot ½in (1cm) larger than the original pot.

Remember always that if we require top growth on our plants it is necessary to ensure that there is room for root growth within each pot.

Examining Biennial Plants

Those growers particularly keen on showing their plants will probably have taken the cuttings which will develop into their show plants in late spring or early summer of the previous year. These plants will have been growing steadily throughout the summer, autumn and winter, and should now be vibrant with growing energy. A continuation of the training of these plants will be necessary and it will be vital to ensure that no damage is caused to the framework of the plant. Any dead or dying leaves must be removed from within the dense branches and foliage – failure to do so often results in a branch being lost when botrytis takes a hold.

Regular feeding with a balanced feed will be essential to ensure that steady growth is maintained. Regular examination of the root ball will tell you

BEWARE 'JACK FROST'

It is very easy, especially in the early part of spring, to assume that the fears of frost have passed. Two or three days of balmy, warm spring weather can lull us into a false sense of security. Be ready to give additional warmth in the greenhouse when night frosts are forecast. If the greenhouse is so full of plants that some have to be housed in outdoor frames then it is important to ensure that protective covering is available. Horticultural fleece is excellent for this purpose – it is light and a double thickness will raise the temperature by two or three degrees.

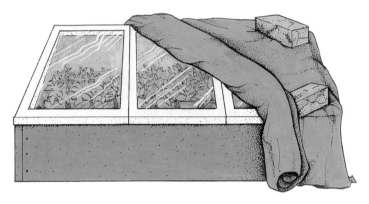

Conversely during spring we are often blessed with warm, sunny days. The temperature within a closed greenhouse will soar and it will be absolutely vital to ensure that as much ventilation as possible is given, and that the plants are kept as cool as possible. Shading, even very early in spring, is a necessity to prevent the very hot rays of the sun through the glass scorching our somewhat tender plants.

In summary, beware the extremes of temperature so often experienced during this exciting time of the year.

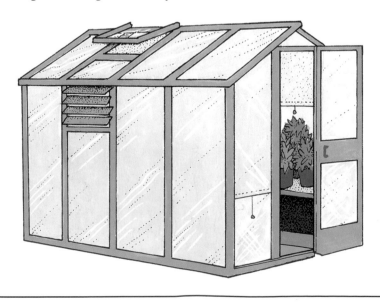

when it is necessary to provide additional nutrients in the shape of fresh compost. Regular turning of each plant to encourage even and symmetrical growth must become a regular routine.

Taking of Cuttings

The method by which cuttings are taken from plants and rooted has been dealt with in greater detail in Chapter 3. Any soft young growth, preferably soft green tips, can be used as cuttings and at this time of the year such growth is in abundance. I prefer to treat the shaping of the plants and the taking of cuttings as tasks which can be performed at the same time. The removal of small growing tips will encourage the development of more shoots on the plant and will at the same time provide material which can root and develop into new plants.

The Hardy Border

Plants which were placed in their permanent beds in the hardy border the previous summer should have come through the winter quite successfully. If the advice to plant fairly large plants so that the root system is a few inches beneath the surface of the surrounding soil was followed then the roots should have been sufficiently insulated. In early spring it is exciting to be able to forage amongst last year's stems in the hope of finding new shoots breaking through the surface. Do not be tempted to remove the 'old' top growth too quickly – it will still give some protection from late frosts.

A window display of tender fuchsias.

Ruthless pruning of hardy plants growing in a permanent site in the garden (right).

When you are satisfied that the risk of further frosts is minimal then the old top growth should be pruned completely away. Unless you are trying to develop a fuchsia hedge then new growth that appears in the upper parts of the old stems will not be needed. When pruning has been completed a feed by sprinkling some general fertilizer around the base of each plant will be of value to encourage the strong new growth, a mulch with a few handfuls of compost is also beneficial.

If it is your intention to plant a new hardy border during the current year then it will be sensible to ensure that the ground is in good heart by digging in some slow-release general fertilizer. Do not be tempted to plant our your new plants until all risk of frost has passed. Perhaps it would even be best to describe this as being an early summer job.

*'Corallina' will make a good hedge.
Plant out in early summer.*

*Planting a Fuchsia Hedge.
The hedge should be planted in soil
that has been deeply dug in advance
and to which the addition of a good,
slow-release fertilizer has been made.
Dig out a trench the depth of the
plants' rootballs plus 2in (5cm). Place
the plants in the base of the trench
18in (45cm) apart. Remember that as
with all outdoor plants, it will be
necessary to provide the plant crowns
with a dressing of insulating material
for the winter (below).*

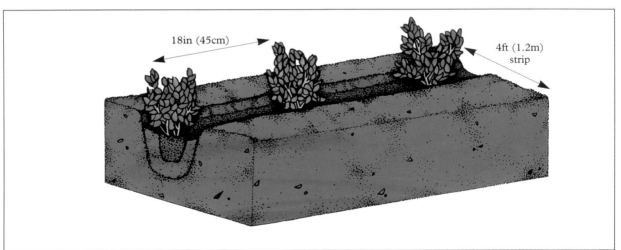

Standards

It is to be hoped that all your overwintered Standards have come safely through. The top growths of those plants that were allowed to go completely dormant should be pruned back quite severely – leaving 6–9in (15–22cm) on each branch will ensure a fairly tight head. We now need to encourage growth of young buds as soon as possible so a regular spraying with tepid water is the order of the day. A temperature in excess of 40°F (4–5°C) should be maintained to encourage the development of the buds. Feeding with a high nitrogen feed will also assist, but be careful not to overwater the compost. When the first pink buds are visible then some judicious pruning of the root system can be undertaken. If the bottom 3–4in (8–10cm) of compost is removed and fresh compost placed in the pot this will give the roots additional space in which to grow. It might also be sensible to take the opportunity of replacing the stake with a fresh one for the coming season.

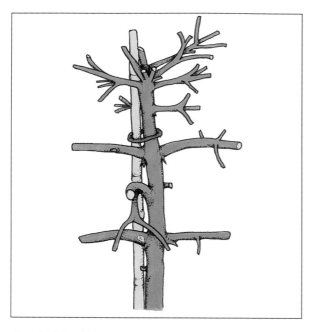

Standard heads should also be pruned back quite hard in order to encourage new vigorous growth.

'Alan Ayckbourne' is well suited to training as a standard.

Plants which have been overwintered in 'green leaf' will be growing apace as soon as the temperature rises. Maintain the feeding with a high nitrogen feed and also pinch out the growing tips of each branch as soon as two or three sets of leaves have developed. Time spent in shaping the plant now will repay handsome dividends later.

TIP

If you find that the growth of buds is very uneven, this can often be corrected by lying the standard on its side with the bare branches uppermost.

Hanging Baskets or Containers

As early as possible in the spring it is important to make up your baskets. Do not be tempted to hang them outside but give them a favoured position within a greenhouse to build up into a large structure. Baskets made from new plants grown from cuttings taken in the autumn will rapidly expand to fill the whole of the basket. Continue with the pinching out of the growing tips (when three sets of

'Whickham Beauty' a strong, upright fuchsia whose slightly lax growth lends itself well to training as an excellent weeping standard.

leaves have formed) and try to encourage the growth to grow outwards and to cascade over the edge of the container.

'Susan Olcese' is extremely good for growing in the basket or hanging container.

'Pink La Campanella', an excellent subject for patio container growing.

Watering and Feeding

During spring it is important that the watering and feeding of our plants is carried out with great care. As is well known fuchsia plants like to have a moistness around their roots but abhor wetness. Provided that the compost that you have used is a well drained one then any water poured onto the surface of the compost will rapidly soak down through, moistening all parts of the pot, but any excess will drain away. If your preference is for watering from below – that is standing the pot in a saucer of water – allow about fifteen minutes for the compost to take up as much moisture as is needed by capillary action, and then remove the excess from the saucer. Do not have your plants standing in water. The drainage holes in the bottom of pots allow the water to drain out but also allow the entry of air. Standing pots in water prevents this intake of air, the roots will be unable to breathe and drowning and the subsequent death of the roots will follow.

Fuchsias, being gross feeders, will require additional nutrients to those available in the compost within a couple of weeks of potting on. The types of feed which are soluble in water – and I recommend the Chempak Liquid Feeds – are very useful indeed. It has often been recommended that in the early part of a plant's growing cycle a feed containing a higher percentage of nitrogen should be given. The high nitrogen will encourage the rapid growth of the foliage and the development of the plant. My personal preference has changed slightly over the last few years and I am now recommending a balanced feed throughout the year. Chempak No. 3 (with an analysis of N20 P20 K20) is the one I now use.

'Antigone' a well-established cultivar that is still very popular.

However, there are many excellent feeds available and experimentation is necessary to determine which is the one best suited to your needs.

Many growers are now using the slow-release fertilizers that are available in pellet or cone form. These are excellent but I do feel that they need to be supplemented, occasionally, with a dilute, balanced, liquid feed.

SUMMER

Keeping Cool

One of the major problems experienced by all growers during the summer months is that of keeping the plants as cool as possible. It is very noticeable that when the temperature rises above a certain mark the plants give the impression of not wanting to do any more growing. My observations are that temperatures above 80–82°F (28°C) will have this effect. How then can we reduce the problem and how can we keep the temperature as low as possible?

If at all possible no plants should be under glass but, having said that, sometimes there is no alternative. Shading of glass with white emulsion paint or a substance such as Coolglass will help to reduce the temperature dramatically, the hot rays of the sun being reflected away. Shading with green netting, preferably attached to the outside of the house, will also be of considerable assistance.

The full, and very distinctive blooms of 'Impulse'.

Many growers remove some of the glass panels to encourage a greater circulation of air – certainly doors and windows should be open as fully as possible to encourage maximum air movement. Taking this idea a stage further it is possible to have 'shade houses'. These are structures with a simple timber framework covered with mesh netting. This will give a good shading from the sun and also, in the event of heavy showers of rain, break the large drops into a fine spray of water droplets.

Since evaporation of water will cause a lowering of temperature then the damping of the floor, staging and surrounds of the greenhouse will help to keep the temperature under control.

Watering of the plants when they appear to be wilting might not always be a good thing as the wilting might easily be caused by the heat, rather than dryness around the root system. Instead, spraying overhead with a fine mist will have the desired effect of helping the plants to perk up.

As stated at the beginning of this section it is far better if the plants are outside but even then, especially if they are being grown in pots, they can suffer from excessively high temperatures. A shaded spot away from the direct rays of the sun, under trees for example, is certainly a favoured and welcome site.

A great deal of our problems are caused because of the direct heat on the compost contained within thin plastic pots. Plants grown in the old-fashioned clay pots do not suffer in quite the same way. One of the methods to overcome this heat is by 'double-glazing' the pots. A misnomer perhaps, but if you can imagine the pot containing the plant being placed inside a larger pot and the space between the two being filled by an insulating material, you will see what I mean.

It is probably fair to say that there are more difficulties in keeping plants cool than there are in keeping them free of frost during severe winters.

Feeding

One rule worth repeating is that one should not feed a plant that is dry at the roots. It is always advisable to give plants a good watering before giving a second watering which incorporates the feed. Feeding your plants each time you water them is a method strongly recommended these days. Most of us suffer from lapses of memory and it is sometimes difficult to remember when feeding was last carried out. Feeding with a liquid feed at a quarter of the usual recommended strength will ensure that the nutrient level of the compost is kept at the correct level. Again, it might be a good idea, having fed with four consecutive feeds, to water with pure water for the fifth day. This will then wash away any excessive salts that might be building up within the compost.

Damping of the greenhouse floor, staging and surrounds will help to keep the temperature down.

'Poppet' does well in full sun.

'Orange Flare', another sun-loving cultivar.

OVERFEEDING

It is an ill advised gardener who, having realized that a feed had been missed, doubles the strength on the next occasion. I suppose the best comparison that can be made would be the unpleasantness of indigestion experienced by people after over-indulging at a meal.

Watering

One of the penalties that we incur when we attempt to grow too many plants is that we are unable to treat each as an individual, and when watering has to be done each and every plant is given the same treatment irrespective of the need. In a perfect setting we would be able to lift each plant, assess its needs, and water accordingly. But we do not live in a perfect world. Having said this, try to handle your plants as regularly as possible, noting any idiosyncrasies, such as an objection to being severely pinched. If a certain plant doesn't seem to want to grow for you – in spite of its growing like a weed next door – do not despair: you can try again next year, or far better really, decide to concentrate on those plants that do grow well for you.

Unfortunately the symptoms displayed by a plant suffering from overwatering are virtually identical with those of a plant which requires water. If a plant is showing signs of wilting pick it up. If the pot feels light in weight then a shortage of water is indicted. But if the pot feels heavy then overwatering will be the cause – the root system drowning – and drastic action will be necessary. Remove the plant from the pot and stand the root ball on the upturned pot in the hope that the excess water will rapidly drain away and the plant recover. An examination of the root ball will probably indicate a mass of dark brown, unhealthy looking (healthy roots are white) roots. If the plant does not make a slight recovery after a couple of hours it will be necessary to remove as much of the old compost as possible and to repot into fresh compost. A pruning of the root system to remove any obvious dead roots will also be necessary. After repotting, the plant should be treated as an invalid, kept in the cool, sprayed from above, and given a minimum of water to enable the root system to be just moist. Hopefully the plant will recover.

WATERING AND GLASS

Take care with the watering of plants in green-houses: remember that water droplets on leaves and flowers will magnify the sun's rays shining through the glass, resulting in unsightly scorch marks.

The semi-double 'Vivienne Thompson'.

The tender, large-flowered F. boliviana, *classified as a climbing plant and best grown with as much root room as possible in a conservatory or greenhouse border.*

Biennial Plants

During the very early days of summer, before the hottest part of the year, it will be possible to think ahead and to decide about the plants that you require, perhaps for show purposes, for next year. Fuchsias are really perennial plants and will keep growing from year to year, but to obtain large spec-imens showing their first flushes of fresh flowers, it is best to treat fuchsias as though they were biennials – that is, growing the plants one year to produce their flowers the next – and take cuttings now.

Fuchsia cuttings require just moisture and warmth in order to root. Our problem therefore will again be to keep the cuttings as cool as possible so that they are warm and not *hot*. In more temperate climates the temperature during late spring

BIENNIAL CUTTINGS

If the conditions that you are able to offer your plants during the winter are conducive to continuous steady growth, you might consider growing some plants on the biennial method. Briefly, this is growing the plants one year and flowering them the next. You will require a minimum temperature of 40–45°F (7–8°C) to be maintained throughout the winter and this could be costly – the larger plants you see on the show bench are grown by this method. You will need to take cuttings of your plants to be grown this way now. Soft tip cuttings are best to use and they can be as small as you like. Choose only those varieties that you wish to have on the show bench. They will need no bottom heat for rooting and can be treated quite severely throughout their initial growth. If cuttings have rooted before the end of late spring pot them into small pots – 3in (7.5cm) would be ideal – and let them grow on steadily. It will be necessary to start the training of these plants at a very early stage, and within a few weeks of rooting, when two pairs of leaves have been formed, the growing tips should be removed. The branching process will have started, and these plants will not be allowed to flower this year.

'Blue Waves' has upright, bushy growth and double blooms. It is easy to grow, a good exhibition plant, and one that can be grown by the biennial method.

and early summer is such that cuttings can be rooted easily without any additional artificial warmth.

Once rooted these young plants are encouraged to grow very steadily through the first summer and autumn, the growing tips of each shoot being removed when one or two sets of leaves have been formed. A very dense canopy of branches will therefore build up which will give innumerable flower-bearing shoots for next year. Steady growth, not rapid growth, is what is required, so regularly feeding with a balanced feed as opposed to a high nitrogen feed will be the order of the day.

These plants should be grown out of doors – standing in fairly long grass will give them a lovely cool and moist environment which they will greatly appreciate. Care will be needed to ensure that with the denseness of the foliage botrytis does not make a foothold.

Training your Plants

Returning now to the plants that we are growing for flowering in the current year we should still be continuing the process of training our plants and encouraging the young growths to position themselves where we would like them to be. To form a

'Earl of Beaconsfield', another cultivar that requires early stopping to encourage shapely growth.

good bushy plant we need to encourage the growth of as many branches as possible. Each time we take out the growing tip from a shoot all the young buds in the leaf axils on that stem will start to grow. If there were three sets of leaves then the one branch will start to develop a minimum of six new branches or laterals. When 'stopping' a plant make sure that each and every growing tip is removed – leaving just one growing tip will ensure that all the strength and vigour of the plant will be concentrated on that one shoot and uneven growth will be the result.

Plants for the Patio

Fuchsias are fantastic value when grown in patio tubs. Any type can be grown (after all the early part of their growing can be undercover if you wish) and it is possible to break show rules in order to get a

WHEN TO STOP STOPPING

We can continue taking out the growing tips and placing the plants in larger pots right through the year if we wish. We will, however, finish up with a huge plant covered in foliage but without any flowers. The object of the exercise is to have as many flowers as possible so there comes a time when the 'stopping' must stop. A plant which has single flowers will require approximately eight weeks from its final 'stopping' to produce its flowers.

A double-flowered plant (that is one with eight or more petals in the corolla) will require at least another two weeks making a total of ten weeks from the final 'stop'. Some of the species and the triphylla fuchsias require even longer to produce their flowers. If it is necessary that your plants should be in flower for a specific day then the necessary final stopping will have to be calculated accordingly. Unfortunately this is not an exact science and the 'stopping dates' can only be very approximate. There are so many variables that affect the timing, such as a spell of hot weather or a spell of dull, damp weather, and different cultivars even if all 'singles', can need different amounts of time. A sound idea would be to keep a record of the stopping dates and the subsequent flowering dates of each of the cultivars you wish to grow for show.

good display. When growing plants for showing on the showbench the rules always stipulate that each pot should contain just one plant (the exceptions being for baskets and hanging pots). However, when growing plants for a patio tub we can grow any number we like together in order to get a mass of foliage and flower. This is actually the method of display used by nurserymen at major shows. Three plants growing strongly in 3½in (9cm) pots can be placed in a patio tub early in the season and the resultant growth will so intermingle that the impression will be given of just one large plant growing happily in the pot. More than three plants can be used if you wish but I feel that this number will give each plant plenty of space to form a good root system, and thus top growth, within the confines of the patio tub.

'Susan Green' makes a superb basket, and can also be trained as a weeping standard.

Once in position the plants are treated as though they were just one plant and fed and watered accordingly. Fuchsias alone in a patio tub can look very effective but they can be enhanced with the use of other low growing bedding plants around the base of the taller growing fuchsias. There is no reason why three or four low-growing, perhaps foliage type fuchsias (*F. autumnale* would be ideal), be positioned around the edge.

The Hardy Border

When all risk of frost has passed it is possible to plant out some hardy fuchsias in their permanent beds. Plants which were grown from cuttings taken in the autumn should be of sufficient size. They should be 'hardened off' so that the shock of being transferred from the cosseted enclosure of the greenhouse will not be too severe.

Once the fuchsia are planted in the border, keep an eye open for pests and diseases, especially if the border is in fairly close proximity to trees. Capsid bugs can cause untold damage to the young growing shoots and greenfly seem to appear from nowhere. Regularly spraying (easier on outdoor plants) will keep both of these pests at bay.

PLANTING OUT HARDY FUCHSIAS

1. Prepare the ground well and rake some long-lasting fertilizer such as bone meal into the soil.
2. With a fairly wide border it is perhaps better to plant your fuchsias in groups of three. This will give a superb mound of foliage and flowers even in the first season. However, in a narrow border, plants can be placed singly at a distance of about 18in (45cm) to 2ft (60cm) from each other. Plant them deeply – if the top of the compost from the pot is roughly 2–3in (5–8cm) below the surface of the soil then the roots will be well insulated from the frosts during their first winter.
3. Once planted the fuchsias in the border should not be neglected. In dry spells watering will be necessary and a continuation of a feeding programme – a balanced feed once a week – will have the desired effect of building up superb plants.

'Maureen Ward', a natural trailer which makes an excellent basket subject.

Hanging Pots and Baskets

One of the nicest ways of looking at fuchsias is looking up at them. Hanging baskets and pots are ideal for this purpose. A number of plants of the same cultivar can be placed in any hanging container that you wish to use; I specifically state 'of the same cultivar' as it is important that the foliage grows uniformly and that the flowers appear at the same time. If cultivars are mixed, uneven growth and irregular flowering often occurs. Five or six plants in a basket of 12in (30cm) diameter will fill it very adequately and more or fewer can be used according to the actual size of your container.

SEED PODS

Throughout the spring and summer months, you will remove seed pods and dead flowers in order to encourage your plants to produce more flowers. Do not, however, be tempted to sow the seed from the seed pods you remove: although you will know the parentage of the seed-bearing plant, you will not know the pollen bearer. It would be extremely good luck if you obtained anything really worth while from seeds, and much time, effort and space will have been wasted in the process.

Many people, and I count myself amongst them, like to see baskets filled with flowers of all types, as there are so many beautiful plants from which we can choose. The fuchsia perfectionists would say that fuchsias alone make the best baskets and yet

'Carmen Maria', a sport of 'Leonora', is a popular choice for the show bench.

The Encliandra-*type 'Radings Inge' has 'perfect' blooms and spreading, but strong, growth. It looks very well in mixed tubs or baskets and is a popular exhibition plant.*

fuchsias when growing strongly in a mixed basket are enhanced by and will enhance other plants.

As with the plants in the garden, remember to remove all spent flowers, seed pods and yellowing leaves. If a plant looks a little sickly, examine it carefully for red spider mite or greenfly.

Regular feeding and watering throughout the season is an essential duty when growing baskets. The combination of sun and wind will dry them out very quickly and it is often necessary to give a good watering twice or more each day. The use of water-retaining crystals will help to reduce the amount of watering but it will still be necessary to keep a very careful watch on the situation.

Attending Shows

Towards the end of the summer and into autumn it is possible to attend specialist fuchsia shows to see how the real 'experts' and enthusiasts grow their plants. A lot can be learned from talking to the exhibitors; strangely, with the fuchsia-growing fraternity there does not appear to be the veil of secrecy which so often surrounds the growing and exhibiting of other plants.

Try to visit as many shows or displays as possible and always go armed with a notebook. Note the names of those plants which attract your attention – not necessarily the prize winners. Note, if you can, the names of the exhibitors, and bear in mind that a quiet word of appreciation for their plants will often bring the offer of a young plant in the spring.

If you have the impression that plants which you have at home are the equal of those on the show bench, be determined that the following year your own plants will also be displayed on the benches. Who knows – one of them might well finish up wearing the red ribbon for being the best plant in the show.

'Katrina Thompsen', trained as a miniature standard for the show bench.

PRESENTATION OF SHOW PLANTS

If you have been growing plants for show, you will have invested a considerable amount of time and effort into their care and development, so it is worth while making sure that on the day of the show you present your plants to their best possible advantage. Competition is keen, and it would be heartbreaking to find that a preventable flaw in an otherwise splendid specimen has ruined its chances.

❀ Any canes or ties you use to support your branches (which will be heavily laden with flowers) should be as inconspicuous as possible.

❀ Make sure that the plant is pest-free. Use insecticide pins or a systemic insecticide watered into the compost. (Do not spray on open flowers or well developed buds or they will be severely stained.)

❀ Any powder residues from feeds that you may have used should be carefully removed from the leaves.

❀ Examine all you plants carefully before leaving them on the show bench in an effort to find any seed pods hiding amongst the foliage. If possible enlist the help of someone else with this, as a fresh eye is often invaluable.

❀ Finally, when the plants are staged, spray with clear water to give them a sprightly look.

❀ Make sure that you arrive at the show in plenty of time so that you are not obliged to rush your inspection and final adjustments.

AUTUMN

This is one of the nicest seasons of the year for sitting back and enjoying the beauty of our plants. However, during our day-dreaming perhaps we can be thinking ahead to what we will need to do to ensure that our plants come safely through the winter and how we can start to prepare for the seasons ahead of us.

Feeding

We should be continuing to feed our plants in order to build up good healthy stock to come through the ordeals of the winter. Plants which you intend to rest can be given feeds containing a higher proportion of potash, which will have the effect of

PROLONGING FLOWERING

My desire is always to prolong the flowering time of my plants which are growing in either pots or hanging containers as long as possible. High potash tends to slow down and perhaps stop the further production of flower buds. To counteract this possibility I continue to feed with a balanced fertilizer such as Chempak No. 3 (20.20.20) right the way through the season. With luck and safety from frosts, flowering can continue well into the winter months.

The large, full and freely produced double blooms of 'Jim Dodge', an excellent choice for the hanging basket.

Remember to take cuttings from hardy plants in the garden as an insurance policy against their not surviving the winter.

ripening the wood. It has often been recommended that a higher potash feed should be given when the buds on our plants start to show colour and that the depth of colour thus achieved is far greater. A feed such as Chempak No. 4, Phostrogen, Tomorite, or Vitax 103 will be admirably suitable for this purpose.

The Hardy Border

Plants in the hardy border will still be flowering profusely for several more weeks – in fact until the first severe frosts arrive. As the season of autumn progresses it is quite amazing how the plants in the hardy border benefit from the moistness of morning dews and the heavy mists. In fact, when you look at the plants, you could be forgiven for believing that we were back in spring. Fresh, young, soft, green growths appear at the ends of the branches and some of the more mature shoots lower down on the plants are still producing their flowers in quantity. But it is to the soft green tips of the shoots that I will be paying the most attention, as they are so similar to the sort of shoots that we used during the spring as cuttings. There lies the answer – cuttings taken now from these 'hardy' plants will root quite easily, grow steadily through the winter, and will be ideal young plants for replacing any plants that do not come safely through the winter. The method of taking such cuttings is described in greater detail in chapter 3, but the main thing is not to rush the rooting process. In fact the coolest possible position should be found for the propagators – it will not matter if it takes six or more weeks for the rooting to start. Once rooting has taken place the cuttings can remain within their propagators where slow steady growth can be encouraged. If they begin to grow so well that they are finding their

The vivid blooms of the hardy 'Reading Show', which are freely produced throughout the season. A good choice for the hardy border.

Hanging Baskets

Although our hanging baskets are probably looking rather jaded towards the end of autumn they still have a very useful part to play. It is perhaps wise to think carefully about the success of the baskets during the coming season and to decide whether a change of position might suit them better. Decide also, if you have experimented with slow-release food pellets and water-retaining gels, whether they have been a success.

Thoughts should be going ahead to next year and the opportunity should be taken to increase the number of plants by propagating from those which have given so much pleasure. Small shoots without

The striking 'General Monk', ideal for the border.

quarters somewhat cramped they can be removed from the propagators and their tips removed to give a fresh batch of cuttings. The 'parent' rooted cuttings can be potted on, given as much light and gentle warmth as possible, and be allowed to continue to grow steadily.

I have often recommended that enthusiasts should try all their favourite plants in the hardy border to see whether or not they will survive the winter weather. This method of taking cuttings in the autumn and growing them on through the winter will act as an insurance policy should any of these favourites be lost.

'Eden Lady', a sister seedling to 'Border Queen', but only semi-hardy.

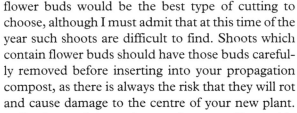

'White Haven', a cross between 'Border Queen', 'Liebriez' and 'Ann H. Tripp'.

flower buds would be the best type of cutting to choose, although I must admit that at this time of the year such shoots are difficult to find. Shoots which contain flower buds should have those buds carefully removed before inserting into your propagation compost, as there is always the risk that they will rot and cause damage to the centre of your new plant.

Cuttings taken and rooted now will provide excellent plants for next year's containers and can be grown steadily, with a minimum of artificial heat, during the winter.

Biennial Plants

Plants which are being grown using the 'biennial' system will need careful looking after during the winter so arrangements should be made during the autumn to ensure that they will continue growing in good condition. Our objective will be to get them into a state of semi-dormancy – still in green leaf but not really growing. To this end the young plants will need ripening. They have been growing

outside since they were first potted on and they can remain there until we are threatened with frosts. Feeding with a balanced feed or one leaning towards the higher potash end of the scale will assist in the wood ripening process.

A close examination of each of the plants will be necessary and this can be done at your leisure as autumn progresses. Dead and dying leaves should be removed from the plants and care must be taken to ensure that there is no debris on the compost. A thorough cleansing of the plants by spraying with a combined insecticide and fungicide will ensure that they are in a clean healthy state.

A decision will need to be made as to where the plants will be placed during the winter and the type of warmth that will be given to them. If you are fortunate in having a small greenhouse, or a partitioned section of a larger house that you can keep heated to a minimum temperature of 40°F (4.5°C), this will be absolutely ideal. Make sure that you will have easy access to the plants and the staging and that all parts are scrupulously cleaned prior to the housing of the plants. This is undoubtedly a job for one of those pleasant but chillier days that we so often experience.

PREPARING THE GREENHOUSE FOR WINTER STORAGE

Many of the comments made in this chapter refer to the preparations necessary for the safe overwintering of our plants. Perhaps the most important factor, one which unfortunately many of us break, is the need for cleanliness within the greenhouse. It would be rather silly to spend a lot of time ensuring that each plant was clean, healthy and free from all pests before bedding them down for the winter if the greenhouse was not in a similar condition. The opportunity should be taken to completely empty the greenhouse, scrub down everything using a good disinfectant, and remove any shading that was painted onto the glass earlier in the year. During the winter months light intensity will be at its lowest and if plants continue to grow under such conditions they will be thin and straggly.

Triphylla-type Fuchsias

Although it is not really necessary to treat your *tri-phylla*-type fuchsias any differently to other cultivars we need to remember that this group of

The triphylla *hybrid, 'Gartenmeister Bonstedt'. Growth is upright and vigorous, and continues late into the autumn.*

fuchsias are particularly frost shy. They can be safely brought through the winter by covering them and protecting them from severe frost but it might be better to emulate the methods adopted by some of the real *triphylla* enthusiasts.

When the show season has finished – late summer or early autumn – the plants should be pruned rather severely, which can be heart-breaking when there are still many flowers on show and the foliage is still excellent. If each of the branches is cut back so that only about 6in (15cm) remains on each it will be possible to thoroughly clean the pot and the surface of the compost. All foliage can be removed from the remaining portion of the stems and then each plant should be given a thorough spraying with a combined insecticide/fungicide. If placed in the protected environment of a greenhouse fresh growth will start to appear on the short stems. Growth will be steady and can be encouraged by spraying and feeding with a balanced liquid fertilizer.

As autumn turns into winter these plants should be placed in the warmest part of the greenhouse – we will be hoping to maintain a temperature of about 45°F (7°C) so that the plants will remain in green leaf but not really growing.

In the spring, plants treated in this way burst into vibrant life, can be given fresh compost into which they will send their active roots, and grow strongly, producing good flowering stems.

Species

More and more enthusiasts are growing a few of the species fuchsias. These are the plants, originally taken from the wild, from which all of our modern cultivars have descended. The treatment that we need to give them is very similar to that given to other plants. Most are extremely frost shy so care must be taken to ensure that they are kept in frost-free conditions.

F. hemsleyana *will grow up to several feet tall in its natural habitat (above).*

One of the species, F. paniculata – *sometimes referred to as the 'Lilac fuchsia' – has strong, upright growth and laurel-like leaves. It is easy to train and is a good species for the beginner.*

Some will want to keep growing during the winter and some will even want to produce their flowers during those colder months. Enthusiasts will be aware of these factors and will endeavour to give their plants the right conditions.

WINTER

I suppose of all the questions asked when displaying at major shows the one most frequently posed is, 'How do we look after our plants during the Winter?' We should always remember that fuchsias are fairly tender plants and will not tolerate severe frost. Following a severe frost plants which have been affected will be completely defoliated and there may even be damage to the main structure of the branches. With a prolonged spell of cold weather all top growth is likely to be completely killed. However if the root system is protected from the frost, either by being some distance beneath the surface of the soil or within a building, it is unlikely to be affected and when moisture and warmth increase in the spring it will produce fresh young shoots to replace those which were lost.

The basic rule that we must try to obey is that we must keep our plants frost-free and the root system just moist.

The very distinctive, semi-hardy 'Space Shuttle', which is most unusual in that it flowers all year round.

Pot Plants

Plants which are in pots, especially thin plastic pots, will have little insulation for the root system if left outside. Some means of wrapping them up for the winter therefore needs to be devised. A lot will depend upon the number and the size of the plants that you wish to overwinter. With just a small number a large box with some insulating material surrounding each of the pots in an unheated shed will probably suffice. The same container in a spare room will be very satisfactory. With a greater number, if an unheated greenhouse is available, it is possible to pack a great number together and surround them with an insulating material such as polystyrene chips, newspapers, roof insulating material or anything else which has the same qualities.

'Santa Claus', a hardy cultivar with semi-double, striking blooms.

Preparation for the winter storage is something which needs to be considered carefully. Plants in pots will have been growing well during the last couple of seasons and will have made a considerable amount of top growth. Such growth makes plants difficult to

'Lady Boothby', a hardy cultivar with upright, vigorous growth.

OVERWINTERING POT PLANTS

Before storing a plant for the winter, ensure that it is healthy, and, if not, take the necessary remedial action: there is little point in overwintering a sickly or pest-ridden plant.

❀ Prune the top growth from the plants and remove any leaves and debris from the surface of the compost. Spray the defoliated, pruned plants with a combined insecticide/fungicide and then allow them to dry in the open air. (If branches are damped when they are stored the risk of their rotting is increased.)

❀ If the temperature of their winter quarters is likely to be below 35°F (1–2°C), insulate the plants with a suitable material before packing them closely together in their storage container.

At regular intervals throughout the winter, it is necessary to unpack and inspect the plants; if the compost is found to be very dry it should be dampened before being returned to storage. Towards the end of winter, the conditions may be such that the plants begin to show signs of growth; otherwise it will be necessary to provide some artificial heat to start them off. (See the 'Pruning for new growth and potting back' in the spring section of this chapter.)

pack away so it will be necessary to reduce the size of the plants quite considerably. If the plants are left outside until the first frost then the task of defoliating the plants will be done for us, otherwise you should remove the foliage yourself. The top growths need to be reduced so that each branch is about 6in (15cm) long. All leaves should be removed as well as any debris on the surface of the compost. When all plants have been treated in this way they should be given a very thorough spraying with a combined insecticide/fungicide and then allowed to dry in the open air before being packed closely together in your storage

area. Our aim will be to ensure that the plants are completely free of any pests and diseases – it would be a pity to take unclean plants into a greenhouse which was made squeaky clean earlier.

The insulating material should enclose each pot, although during the course of the season when examination of the plants takes place and those looking rather dry are given a drink of water this material is likely to be displaced.

If you are able to maintain a minimum temperature of approximately 35°F (1–2°C) within a greenhouse then there will be no need to insulate the

BURYING PLANTS

If you have sufficient energy and space to carry out this process, it is a satisfactory method of over-wintering pot plants in the garden, and has the advantage that the plants' rootballs will remain moist.

1. Prepare the plants for burying by gently pruning the defoliated branches and spraying with a combined fungicide and insecticide.

2. Lay the plants, to a depth of about 2½ft (75cm) and line the base with insulating material such as peat, bracken or straw (below).

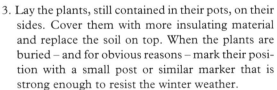

3. Lay the plants, still contained in their pots, on their sides. Cover them with more insulating material and replace the soil on top. When the plants are buried – and for obvious reasons – mark their position with a small post or similar marker that is strong enough to resist the winter weather.

4. In early spring, the plants can be carefully disinterred from their 'grave'. Long white shoots are often found to be growing from the branches, which is a good sign as it indicates that the plants are alive. However, these shoots should be pruned away along with any dead branches. *See* the features on pruning and potting back earlier in this chapter.

individual plants. Bubble film on the inside of the greenhouse will help to maintain a minimum temperature which is frost free and keep the expense of heating as low as possible.

Patio Tubs

The root systems of plants grown in patio tubs will, during severe spells of frost, be attacked from all sides and will need some protection. However, patio tubs are generally sturdier than normal pots so some protection is already given to the root systems. A frost-free cold greenhouse or a shed will be suitable for storing these containers and I would recommend that an 'overcoat' of roof insulation material be wrapped around each container to keep them frost free. It is easier to ensure that such containers are kept in a 'just moist' condition during the winter months.

Hanging Baskets

The same comments regarding the all-round vulnerability of patio tubs applies to hanging contain-

The interesting foliage of 'Sharpitor', a hardy fuchsia that should survive the winter outside. However, it is a slow grower and difficult to propagate. It is best suited to the more experienced fuchsia grower.

ers. There are two main ways of dealing with the plants in the container – we can remove the individual plants from the container and treat each as separate plants or we can try to store the whole basket structure. The former method is perhaps the most successful as each plant when potted on into a separate pot can be looked after as an individual. However, many growers like to build up their baskets and grow them on from year to year. The plants should still be individually pruned and all foliage and any debris which has built up in the basket should be removed. A combined insecticide/fungicide spray will ensure that the plants are clean. The containers can be wrapped in an insulating material and kept either in a frost free shed or a greenhouse where the temperature will remain above freezing point. In the spring, when fresh growth starts, the complete ball of soil in the basket can be lifted, a portion of it removed, and fresh compost added to give sufficient nutrients to commence the growth of new shoots.

Hardy Border

Have you taken out your insurance policy to ensure that you do not lose any of the plants that you have in the hardy border? Have you followed the suggestion under the autumn notes to take young cuttings? If you have then your activities to protect your hardy border plants need only be minimal.

It is assumed that when the plants were first placed in position they were planted quite deeply so that the root system would be protected from severe frosts by the insulating qualities of the soil. This being so, only small amounts of insulating material will be necessary in addition. When we have experienced the first severe frost the foliage will rapidly look sick and will fall to the ground leaving bare stems. The dying foliage should be removed so that any lurking pests or diseases do not remain within close proximity to the plants. The top growths, now denuded of any foliage, can be trimmed back very slightly, just for neatness. The majority of the branches should be left in position as they will give some protection from frosts and will also assist in keeping insulating material in position. Two or three handfuls of a peat-free compost (I use the compost sold in peat-free grow bags) scattered around the crown of each plant will give further protection to the root system.

Nothing more needs to be done other than to inspect the plants regularly and to replace any of the insulating material scratched away by birds. In spring fresh growths should come from the root system and we will take further action when all risks of frost have passed.

Standards

One of the problems associated with standards is overwintering. It has taken a reasonably long time to grow the stem and build up the head of a standard, and it would be a pity if all that time and energy were wasted.

With a standard we have three very vulnerable places. The root system, the stem and the head.

The root system we can protect in the manner already suggested by insulating the pot. The stem creates rather more of a problem, although one simple solution would be to encase it in the type of insu-

'Genii' is a superb border plant and will survive the winter outside, but do not be tempted to leave container plants outdoors regardless of their hardiness. All pot plants require a frost-free environment for the winter.

Check outside plants regularly throughout the winter to ensure that the insulating material is still in place. Renew it if necessary. Apart from peat-free compost, you can use well-weathered ashes or bracken for insulation.

'Bland's New Striped' has upright, self-branching, bushy growth. It makes an excellent standard or pot plant.

'Mission Bells' is sometimes used as a summer bedder, but it is not hardy and is unlikely to survive the winter outside.

lating material used for water pipes. This will fit snugly around the stem and can be tied in position. We are also very anxious not to lose the branches in the head of our plants so some type of covering – either horticultural fleece or strips of material – wrapped around it should serve the purpose. Before doing so though we must remove all the foliage and also reduce the length of each branch. If you reduce each branch by about a half then you will have some room to manoeuvre in the spring when further shaping can take place. The plant should preferably be kept in a frost-free shed, garage, greenhouse or room. Again the root system needs to be kept just moist. Using this method the standard will be kept in a semi-dormant state. In the spring we will have to hope and pray that the branches will send out fresh shoots quite evenly so that a good balanced head can again be grown.

An alternative to this would be to keep the plant just growing and in green leaf during the whole of the winter. This is a method I favour as one can guarantee evenness of growth. It will be necessary to have a greenhouse kept at a minimum of 35°F (1–2°C) throughout the winter as the objective is to keep the plants in green leaf but not actually growing. In late autumn, before frosts are threatening,

the plants should be pruned back quite severely to about a third of their lengths. Spraying regularly with tepid water will encourage new shoots to grow from the leaf axils. By the time frosts are with us the head should be covered with a mass of small green leaves. Kept within the frost-free greenhouse the young shoots will remain relatively static and will be ready to grow rapidly and evenly when the warmer weather of spring arrives.

STANDARDS IN THE HARDY BORDER

One strong word of warning: if you have used standards to add height to your hardy border do not leave them in the border but bring them in during the winter. The first severe frost will probably kill the stem which has taken so much time and patience to grow. Even if the plant used for the standard is recognized as being a strong hardy type do not leave it out – even the hardy bushes lose their upper branches.

With all of the plants that we are overwintering it will be necessary to carry out a strict regime of inspection. The rootball must not be allowed to become bone dry but should remain just moist. If the weather is on the damp side keep a watchful eye open for the first signs of botrytis (grey mould) on the foliage or stems of the plants.

I am often asked if it is really necessary to go through all this rigmarole just to keep plants from one year to the next. The argument put forward is that the money saved from not heating a greenhouse could be used to purchase a great many plants from specialist nurseries in the spring. I cannot argue with that and I tend to keep the number of overwintered plants to an absolute minimum, but there are bound to be some old faithfuls which it would be a pity to lose. The overwintering of standards is also essential if we wish to add height to the hardy border in the summer.

The number of methods used by growers to overwinter their plants is legion. All will work provided that the root system is kept just moist and the plants kept frost free.

CHAPTER 7

Pests and Diseases

Fuchsia growers are very lucky in that they are not troubled with a great many pests and diseases. The few that are are quite easily controlled, but of course it is far better not to allow such conditions to get hold. Prevention is always better than cure. One of the most important suggestions always made to beginners growing fuchsias is not to grow too many plants. This advice is valid in that, if fewer plants are grown, it becomes possible to handle each of them regularly and so any pests or diseases are detected at a very early stage.

PESTS

Greenfly

Greenfly can usually be seen in clusters around the light green tip of each shoot. They are unmistakable in appearance and cause damage to plants in that they are sap-sucking insects, and this action causes distortion and curling of the young leaves. They are very prolific in their reproductive habits so quick action is advisable. Regular spraying with an insecticide such as 'tumblebug' or 'Spray Day' will keep the greenfly at bay, but I must stress the word regular. There are many old-fashioned remedies for dealing with this pest – if you know one, and it seems to work well for you, then continue to use it.

Whitefly

Whitefly are extremely troublesome and unfortunately the fuchsia seems to be a particular favourite of this pest. These whiteflies are easily seen by looking under the upper leaves of plants. Again, they can be controlled by spraying, but unfortunately the sprays are only effective against the adult flies. The

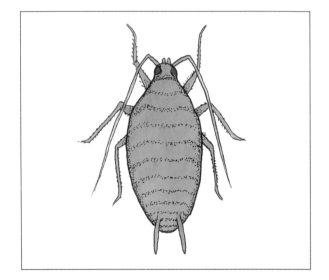

An aphid.

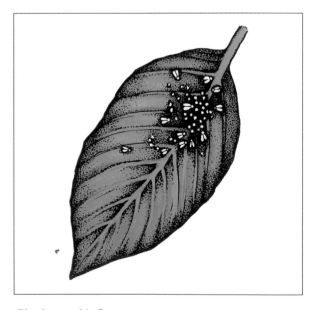

Glasshouse whitefly.

Aphids.

eggs are not affected, so it is necessary to keep spraying at intervals of about four days in order to destroy the newly emerging adults before they can lay further eggs. If a four-day spraying programme is carried out even a severe infection can be eradicated in a couple of weeks. The earlier a possible invasion by whiteflies is discovered, the easier it will be to stamp it out, so regular inspections are the order of the day. When there are only a couple of flies a finger and thumb technique is very satisfactory and satisfying.

It is also possible to introduce a predator, a parasitic wasp *Encarsia formosa*, if the infestation is not too great. The wasp injects its eggs into the whitefly 'scales'. The developing wasp larva then devour the 'scale' as it grows. Unfortunately *Encarsia formosa* will not achieve good control if there is a very heavy infestation. Under those circumstances it will be necessary to spray all plants with a good insecticide to reduce the adult population of whiteflies at least seven days prior to the introduction of the parasitic wasp. It is possible that the parasitic wasp may be introduced into your greenhouse accidentally when purchasing young plants from a nursery where such preventative measures are in operation.

Unfortunately, as with all parasites, there have to be sufficient quantities of the pests present for the parasitic wasp to continue to flourish. Once the population of whitefly has been exterminated the parasitic wasp will also die.

Red Spider

Red spider mites are, I suppose, one of the very worst type of pests for fuchsias. They are very difficult to detect in the early stages and are, in fact, almost invisible to the naked eye throughout their life span. Plants which have been attacked by the red spider mite (not a spider at all really) can be easily recognized, as the foliage turns to a bronze colour and becomes very brittle. In later stages very fine webs can be seen spreading from leaf to leaf.

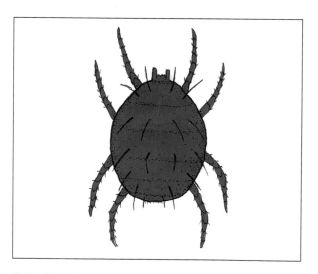

Red spider mite.

This pest is very contagious and rapidly spreads to many plants in a greenhouse. It is often considered that an attack of red spider mite results from poor growing conditions. The mite thrives in a hot, dry atmosphere so if your plants are growing in the correct type of conditions for fuchsias (warm and moist), you are unlikely to suffer severely from it. Plants which are affected should be removed from close proximity to others and thoroughly sprayed with a good systemic insecticide. All plants in the greenhouse should be sprayed regularly.

A predatory mite, *Phytoseiulus persimimilis* can also be introduced into your greenhouse in an attempt to control red spider mite. The predator is orange red in colour, as opposed to the yellow green and dark patches of the red spider mite, and has a pear-shaped body. Both adult and nymph stages of *Phytoseiulus* prey on adults, eggs and nymphs of the red spider mite and are far more active.

Capsid Bug

On plants which are growing outside you may come across another pest which causes disfiguration of the growing tips – the capsid bug. This is another sap-sucking insect which punctures the young leaves, causing them to blister and turn red. Spraying with insecticide will again rectify the position. It is easy to forget the possibility of plants which are bedded out in the garden being attacked, but I am afraid this very often happens, especially if the plants are bedded under, or in close proximity to, larger trees.

Sciarid Flies

Unfortunately with the advent of the soilless (peat-based) composts we seem to have imported these small black flies, which lay their eggs in it. The damage is done by the emerging larvae which will eat the roots of cuttings or seedlings. They rarely affect mature plants, although their presence can be rather annoying. Watering the affected compost with a solution of malathion or stirring some gamma-HCH powder into the top of the compost will have the effect of destroying this pest. Over-watering of peat-based composts encourages the presence of these pests.

Vine Weevil

The vine weevil larva is one pest which seems to have become far more prevalent in recent years, and that prevalence seems to coincide with the advent of peat-based composts. The adult is a black, beetle-like insect and is nocturnal in its habits. The first sign of the presence of the adult vine weevil is when notch-es are seen to have been eaten from the edge of leaves – at first you might feel tempted to blame caterpillars. The greatest damage though is done, not by the adult beetle but by the larvae. The eggs are laid in the surface of the compost and when hatched they produce a grub which is about ½in (1cm) in length, whitish with a brownish head. These grubs burrow down into the compost and feed off the young white roots, doing untold damage to the young plants. Many cures are suggested for vine weevils but malathion soaked into the compost seems to be very effective. Potting back the older plants in the early spring is a good time to discover whether any grubs are present.

The larval (grub) stage of the vine weevil can be controlled in the greenhouse, conservatory or garden, by introducing minute parasitic nematode 'worms' to the soil around infected plants. Nematodes destroy only the grubs and are most effective in late summer when the grubs are still small and before serious damage has been done.

It is also possible to render the eggs of the vine weevil sterile by dousing the compost surrounding each plant with a solution of *Armillatox*. If a dilution rate of 250 to 1 is used (one capful to a gallon of water) regularly during late spring and early summer when adults are active and laying eggs, then some measure of control can be achieved. It is also hoped that the same disinfectant may control and perhaps kill the vine weevil larvae – although the strength necessary for such a purpose has not yet been determined.

Catching and killing the adults by providing hiding places on the greenhouse bench which can be examined regularly also gives some satisfaction.

DISEASES

Botrytis Cineria

Botrytis is one of the two main diseases of which you need to be aware. It is very easily identified by the grey, rather hairy-like mould. This can be caused by dank, airless conditions, the rotting of dying foliage, and a general lack of air circulation. The temptation to grow too many plants too closely packed together promotes the conditions for the growth of this disease. The cure is good circulation of air (vents open

*Some cultivars appear more prone to disease than others.
'Fiona' is one of those that seems to be susceptible to botrytis.*

throughout the year if possible), and the prevention of cold, damp, stagnant conditions. If plants are affected by botrytis then they should be sprayed with a good systemic fungicide or, if the weather is cold and this would only add to the damp conditions, dusted with a fungicide powder.

Rust

Fuchsia rust is another disease which has become far more noticeable in recent years. It is very debilitating and is very easily transmitted from one plant to another. It is readily identified by reddish-brown markings (rings) on the upper side of leaves, while on the underside typical orangey-brown pustules can be seen – in fact, it looks exactly like rust. Unfortunately the spores on the underside of the leaves can be passed from one plant to another purely by the movement of air currents, and also on the hands of the grower or by insects.

The cure for an attack of rust is firstly to remove any infected plants from the presence of other plants. Try to remove any of the leaves which have the tell-tale marks and *burn* them. The whole plant should then be sprayed with a good fungicide such as 'Nimrod T', or 'Plantvax 75' if you can get hold of it. Keep the treated plants separate from others and keep a very careful eye on all plants, removing any infected leaves as soon as the first signs show.

Unfortunately, plants bearing rust spores are sometimes first brought into the greenhouse from the collections of others. It is a wise precaution to place any newly-acquired plants in quarantine for a couple of weeks and thus make sure they are not affected. At one stage experts would have advised the complete burning of any affected plant, but modern methods are not quite so drastic.

The general advice, then, is to spray your affected plants with a suitable insecticide or fungicide. But this is not the only method of removing the offending pests or diseases. In fact, it would be unwise to use wet sprays on your plants when they are in full flower, as the sprays would cause marking and damage to the flowers and buds. I would always recommend using wet sprays at the beginning of the season before buds are well formed, and at the end of the season when plants have been prepared for their winter rests. Always read the instructions very carefully before mixing your sprays. Follow the instructions and do not think that if you use a spray stronger than that recommended you will get better results. You will only be wasting your money, and you could easily damage the foliage of the plants. As most of the sprays only affect the adult pests it will be necessary to undertake a programme of spraying at intervals of three or four days until the infestation has been cleared. Most pests hide themselves under the leaves of the plants so you

Botrytis.

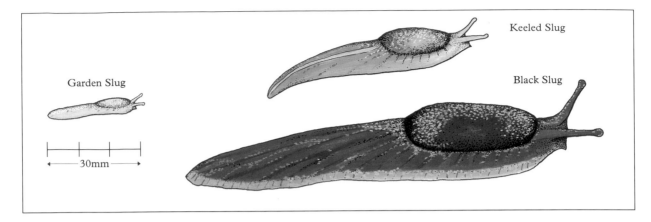

Garden Slug

Keeled Slug

Black Slug

30mm

Fuchsias are also vulnerable to attack from slugs.

must ensure that *all* parts of the plants are well moistened. If the spray you are using is of a systemic variety it will give prolonged protection from the pests or diseases, as the chemical is absorbed through the leaves of the plant and remains in the sap. I would always recommend using a systemic type insecticide or fungicide if one is available.

It is also possible now to obtain insecticide 'pins'. These are pushed into the soil at the base of the plant and the chemical is absorbed by the plant through the root system. This is especially useful when the plants are in flower or if you have just a few special plants for show purposes. It is not the cheapest method of fending off pests, but a simple and very effective one when just a few plants are involved.

It is also possible to purchase 'smoke bombs' or 'cones', which contain a fungicide or insecticide released as a cloud of smoke when they are ignited. These again are very effective at the time of the year when flowers or buds are present, but it does mean closing off the greenhouse and making it as airtight as possible to stop the smoke escaping before the cure has been effected. At the time of the year when we will most need this, the days are likely to be hot and all the ventilation possible is usually being given to the plants. However, if it is possible to carry out the smoking last thing at night, it should be most effective. During damp, cold days in late autumn or early winter, when the atmosphere is heavily laden with moisture and we are anxious not to increase the level of dampness in the greenhouse by spraying, this method of curing the ills is most useful.

NUTRIENT DEFICIENCY

If a plant appears not to be thriving, and you have eliminated pests and diseases as a possible cause, it is likely that the plant is suffering from some nutrient deficiency in the soil. This may occur if the plant has not been potted on regularly or has not been fed sufficiently during the growing season. It may be possible to identify a specific deficiency; for instance, in summer, a yellowing of the leaves may indicate that the plant is deficient in magnesium, in which case a dose of magnesium sulphate will redress the balance.

On the same principle, but advancing a stage further, it is possible to fix up fumigators or vapourizers in your greenhouse. These are rather more expensive but are extremely effective.

If you have only a few plants, and are growing them indoors on the window-sill, don't try to spray whilst they are still indoors. Badly infected plants should be taken outside and given a good spraying. Alternatively, if an infestation is only in its early stages, it is possible to hold the foliage in a bowl of soapy water. This will wash off any aphids which might be present. Insecticide sticks pressed into the compost around the edge of the pot will keep pests at bay.

One final word of warning – keep all chemicals safely locked away. They can be very dangerous to children and to animals. Never keep any 'mixed up' sprays in either bottles or the sprayer – when you have completed your spraying tasks, dispose of the remainder.

CHAPTER 8

More Unusual Fuchsias

SPECIES FUCHSIAS

Amazingly, the fuchsia has been known for less than 300 years. It was in 1703 that the missionary and botanist Father Charles Plumier found the fuchsia in the Dominican Republic and described it. Perhaps even more surprising was the fact that he decided to name it after a sixteenth-century Doctor of Medicine, Leonhard Fuchs. The first fuchsia to be described was *Fuchsia triphylla, flore coccinea.*

Very little was heard of the fuchsia for almost a hundred years after that, but then great strides were made in discovering yet newer species. To date some 102 species have been found and described. Not all are either in, or worthy of, cultivation but a study of the species *fuchsia* is a worthwhile occupation in its own right. The list of species has been broken down into several sections based on the areas in which they were found. Most are indigenous to South America but a few are native to New Zealand and Tahiti.

It is pleasing to note that many more plants of the species are becoming available at specialist fuchsia nurseries and it is hoped that those on offer are correctly named. Many are very easy to grow and are extremely satisfying in that they produce very large bunches of flowers, usually trumpet shaped and of large size. Others produce a mass of very small flowers and it is difficult sometimes to recognize them as being fuchsias. There are yet more which produce their flowers in large corymb panicles, at the ends of laterals, which closely resemble a lilac in full flower. Going from the very large to the very small there are species which produce a mass of very small flowers on long thin spindly stems. And yet another can best be described as a creeping plant in that it travels along the ground, its flowers facing upwards.

General cultivation of these plants does not vary greatly from that of the cultivars. Perhaps the most

important thing is to realize is that the species botanical clocks are set for the southern hemisphere whereas many of us are endeavouring to get them to conform to life in the northern hemisphere. Most of the species are frost tender so it will be necessary to give very adequate protection during the winter months. The other important factor to remember is that, in the wild, their roots are able to wander freely amongst the undergrowth. Most are found in the wooded lower foothills of mountains and will therefore be used to a diet rich in leaf mould. Their root run is not restricted in any way and it is perhaps because we attempt to restrict the roots within pots that difficulties occur. Providing a large pot as the plant develops in size and being very sparse with any

'Bergnimf', an F1 hybrid between F. sessifolia × F. fulgens.

additional feeding will encourage the formation of flower buds as opposed to foliage. Many members of the species also take exception to having the ends of their growing shoots cut off on a regular basis. It is perhaps better to grow the species using a minimum of training, giving them as much root and air room as possible.

In selecting species plants it might be wise to seek the advice of someone already knowledgeable in the art. Many specialist nurseries are now making species available – fortunately those which are easier to grow and are the most attractive in appearance when in full flower. I will make no attempt to try and describe many of the species but will endeavour to tempt you with just a few which should give you success and perhaps the desire to seek out some of the more sophisticated and challenging ones.

My first selection is the one seen more frequently than any other on the show benches – popular also because of the minimal space it demands – *F. procumbens*. This plant is a native of New Zealand and is usually found in the sandy and gravelly areas along the sea shore (a similar type of compost will ensure success). The plant is low growing and sends out long trailing shoots which will form adventitious roots as they travel across the ground. The flowers are very attractive though rather small, being no larger than about ½in (1cm) long. The sepals are dark red and the tube buttercup yellow but there are no petals. The pollen on the anthers is a bright blue and adds to the attraction of the plant.

After the blooms die, seed pods are produced. As with all species it is better to leave the seed pods on the plant and not to remove them as is suggested when growing cultivars. These seed pods grow quite large, like miniature damson plums, and the seed contained within them can, when dry, be sown directly onto compost: a high germination rate is usually obtained. Such seedlings will produce plants which are true *procumbens*.

F. procumbens is very easy to propagate as any small piece, when detached, will root quite easily. This plant can very easily be used to clamber over a rock garden and, unless you are extremely unlucky, will safely come through an average winter if left *in situ*.

My second selection is one which often creates doubts in the minds of those viewing it for the first time – the 'Lilac Fuchsia' *F. paniculata*. In the wild

F. procumbens.

this one grows up to about 9ft (3m) in height so it will be necessary to contain it. Having said that, it also requires sufficient root room in order to make a good plant. The flowers are carried erect on terminal corymb panicles; each flower is only about ½in (1cm) in length but there are a great number of them. The tube and sepals are rose-purple and the petals within the small corolla are lavender. Unlike some species the flowers are produced throughout the year and not just as one flush. Small black shiny seed pods are produced as the flowers pass maturity.

There are no real problems with the cultivation of *F. paniculata* but I would suggest that two or at the most three 'stops' are all that are necessary to get a good bushy plant. A short period of rest during the winter season will revitalize the plant and encourage it to produce even more shoots and flowers the following year. I have found that severe pruning in late autumn has no adverse effect on the plant although I must admit that other growers hold up their hands in horror at the thought.

A plant very similar to *F. paniculata* but lacking its ability to flower continuously is *F. arborescens*, whose flowers are also borne in erect terminal flowering corymb panicles. To encourage flowering it is

F. arborescens.

F. fulgens speciosa.

necessary to be rather sparing on the water as it tends to flower during the 'dry season'.

The most popular of all species on the show-bench, probably because of the size of the flowers and the luxuriousness of the foliage, is *F. fulgens*. This species has a number of variants which all have the same characteristics. The flower is shaped very much like a trumpet with a long thin tube some 2in (5cm) in length. The tube is usually dull scarlet in colour and the smallish sepals are yellowish to greenish with perhaps a hint of red at the base. The petals in the corolla are quite small and are bright red. The flowers are carried in multi-flowered drooping racemes. The leaves, which are very velvety in appearance, are huge – some 3½–6in in length (9–15cm) and approx 2–4in (5–10cm) wide. One of the most interesting factors about this species is that it has a tuberous root not dissimilar to that of a dahlia, and the overwintering can consist of keeping the tuber in a frost-free condition and bringing it back into growth in early spring. You might also see some of these plants with the names *F. fulgens rubra grandiflora* or *F. fulgens gesneriana*.

F. fulgens *var.* gesneriana.

My final selection for the larger flowered species must be *F. boliviana*, *F. boliviana* var. *luxurians* and *F. boliviana* var. *luxurians alba*. Again the flowers are carried in terminal racemes or panicles and each individual flower has a tube some 2½in (6cm) in length, which is pale pink to bright scarlet in colouring. The sepals are also pink and reflex back against the tube. The ¾in (2cm) petals are usually bright scarlet. Again the foliage is very luxurious, with large leaves measuring some 8in (18cm) in length and 5in (13cm) in width. This is a relatively easy plant to grow but will need to be grown in a large pot so that the root system is not too restricted.

There is another group of species which have proved very popular and easy to grow, the *F. encliandra* group, whose flowers are usually less than ½in (1cm) in length. These plants are all very similar to each other and, as a result of much cross-fertilization, there are many different flower colours available. The plants consist of long wil-

F. encliandra ssp. encliandra, *with its 'perfect' blooms and fernlike foliage, is very popular.*

lowy stems but the flowers are borne in profusion. When the flowers are finished the plant can be covered with a mass of small, shiny black seeds, which are quite easy to germinate and make possible the proliferation of different flower colours. One of the nice things about this species is that they grow so fast that it is possible to train them into all sorts of shapes. The art of topiary is not one usually associated with fuchsias but plants of the *encliandra* group can be trained around any type of wire shape with fascinating results.

I have not as yet mentioned what is perhaps the most important group of all – the group from which the hardiness of many of our fuchsias has been achieved – the *F. magellanica* group. A visit to the west coast of England, Wales, Scotland or Ireland will give you the opportunity of seeing hedgerows of fuchsias glowing scarlet. There are again many variants to the *magellanica* group: some have yellow leaves, others variegated foliage and others have flowers which are white or whitish pink. As their original home was along the Magellan Straits it is understandable that they should so enjoy the conditions they find along the Gulf Stream coast. No garden should be without at least one *F. magellanica* as they always give great satisfaction and require a minimum of attention.

It will be appreciated that in this chapter I have not attempted to describe all the fuchsia species that are currently available. I have concentrated on those that I find easy to grow in the hope that I can encourage others to spare a little space for one or more of these beauties. After all it is because of these 'originals' that we are able to enjoy the wonderful colouring and versatility of our present-day cultivars.

TRIPHYLLA-TYPE FUCHSIAS

When the first Fuchsia was introduced in 1703 it was a plant described as *Fuchsia triphylla, Flore coccinea*. Needless to say plants descended from *Fuchsia triphylla* have been responsible for many of our modern hybrids and cultivars. It is also very fortunate that plants carrying this strain are far more tolerant to direct sunlight than other cultivars, particularly those which have been evolved from the *F. magellanica* group of plants.

TAKING TRIPHYLLA CUTTINGS

A slight variation in technique is necessary when taking cuttings.

1. Usually I recommend taking small green tip cuttings removed from the parent plant by severing just above the leaf node; with triphylla cuttings it is preferable to take a rather longer cutting, severing just beneath a leaf node and making very sure that the small buds within each leaf axil are not damaged when the lower leaves are removed.

2. The cutting should be inserted carefully into your usual cutting compost so that a number of the leaf axils are beneath the surface of the compost. Since the cutting is longer than usual, you may wish to make a small hole in the compost to reduce the risk of damage to the cutting. It is hoped that, following rooting, the young shoots in the leaf axils will develop and thus form additional stems. A good bushy plant will be produced providing more terminal flowering shoots for a later date.

3. Water the cuttings with a fine-rose on the watering can.

When 'potting on' the plants use the usual method of encouraging shoots from below the surface of the compost by lowering the plant in the new pot. A small quantity only of fresh compost should be placed in the base of the new, larger, pot and the rootball should be placed upon it. Fresh compost is gently trickled around the sides of the pot so that more of the branches are buried. Additional branches will therefore be encouraged to grow from below the soil surface, creating branches and foliage.

'Brighton Belle', a triphylla *type that makes a good basket subject.*

For summer bedding and for growing as specimen plants for shows or on the patio the *triphylla* hybrids are unequalled. Not only are the bunches of flowers, which are produced at the ends of the branches, very eye-catching, but the delicate purple sheen on the reverse of the leaves adds to the attraction. No more difficulty should be experienced in growing the *triphylla*-type fuchsias than in growing any other cultivar. It is necessary, however, to bear in mind that they are frost shy and will need to be given protection in late spring and early autumn from forecast frost.

All fuchsias are generally considered to be gross feeders and will thrive on a balanced nutritional feed throughout the season. However, the *triphyllas* seem to appreciate a higher nitrogen content in their feed and it is certainly advantageous in the early part of the season when growth is almost visible to feed with a high nitrogen feed. This can be continued throughout the season if you prefer, but many of the leading growers recommend changing over to a balanced feed in late spring. High potash feeds are not recommended for the *triphyllas* and

'Stella Ann', triphylla *type with upright, vigorous growth.*

'Fuchsiarama 91', a triphylla *type that responds well to pinching and will make a good symmetrical shape (right).*

may well be responsible for the excessive lower leaf drop often experienced by many growers.

As stated earlier, *triphyllas* are frost shy and it will be necessary to make arrangements for protection from frosts during the winter months. A temperature of 35°F (2°C) will keep them safe and in a semi-dormant state. Do not, however, allow the compost surrounding the rootball to dry out completely – it needs to remain 'just moist' so that the root system will not dry out and die. Before taking the plants under cover for the winter (and a greenhouse is not essential provided you can maintain frost-free conditions elsewhere) the top growth of each plant should be reduced by about a third. All foliage can be removed and the denuded plants given a good spraying with a combined insecticide/fungicide. It is important to do everything possible to prevent the overwintering of any pests and diseases.

In early spring the plants should be removed from their 'resting' quarters and given a further severe pruning. This time all top growth should be removed so that just 2–3in (5–7.5cm) of each

Severely prune triphylla *plants in early spring.*

branch remains. The treated plants can be given a further precautionary spraying with a combined insecticide/fungicide and placed in a light position in a greenhouse where the temperature is maintained at a minimum 40°F (4°C). Daily spraying with slightly tepid water will soften the buds anxious to develop in each leaf axil. Feeding with a dilute feed which is high in nitrogen will bring the root system back into growth.

When the plant is covered with a mass of lovely young pink buds then the plants can be repotted into a new pot with fresh compost. Remove the plants from the pot and gently tease away as much of the old compost as possible. Removal of the bottom couple of inches of compost will enable you to lower the plant into the new pot. Following the usual repotting process, place the plant in a good light position but protect it from the direct hot rays of the sun until flourishing new growth is evident.

'Thalia', *a tender* triphylla *type whose flowers are produced in great quantity throughout the season. It requires early stopping for best results.*

The striking, bright red flowers of 'Peter Crooks', a perfect triphylla *type whose lax growth makes it suitable for use in hanging containers.*

My apologies if I appear to have been enthusing too much about the *triphyllas* but they are really the most attractive of plants and always cause a great sensation when well grown and exhibited on the showbench. Their heavily laden bunches of long tubed trumpets at the ends of each lateral will bring gasps of envy from other growers. Fortunately more and more of our hybridizers are concentrating of the *triphylla* types as a result of which additional ones are appearing on the shelves each year. New is not necessarily better, however, and most of the early *triphylla* hybrids have proved their worth over many years and are still going strongly. One of the most popular, 'Thalia', was raised in Germany as long ago as 1905 by Bonstedt.

A glance through any specialist fuchsia nursery catalogue usually shows a section devoted to the *triphylla* hybrids. All are well worth growing and will give considerable satisfaction over many years.

'Pipers Vale', *a strong-growing* triphylla *type whose habit is suitable for both upright growing and hanging containers.*

Shaping of the plant can commence as soon as new shoots have developed three sets of leaves. Removal of the growing tips will encourage even greater bushiness, but remember that if you are growing for shows plants of the *triphylla* type require a longer period following their final 'stopping' to be in flower. As many as twelve to fifteen weeks will be necessary so your 'stopping' dates must be adjusted accordingly.

PROBLEM

As with most things, there are bound to be drawbacks with something so outstandingly beautiful and attractive as a *triphylla* fuchsia. They are not only attractive to us but also, to the bane of fuchsia growers, the whitefly. It will be necessary, on a very regular basis, to examine the undersides of the leaves to see if whitefly is present. Fortunately the delightful purple sheen on the reverse makes these little horrors very visible, and regular spraying with a good insecticide or watering in a systemic insecticide will keep your plants clean and healthy.

CHAPTER 9

Recommended Cultivars

ALICE HOFFMAN (Klese 1911)

Semi-double. Tube and sepals rose. Corolla white-veined red. Foliage bronze. Excellent variety for growing in the hardy border.

Annabel (Ryle 1977) Double. Tube and sepals white. Corolla creamy white. Makes an excellent show plant, either as a bush, shrub or grown as a standard. Always an eye catcher. Care must be taken in transportation – the flowers bruise easily.

Ann H Tripp (Clark 1982) Single/semi-double. Tube and sepals white. Corolla white. Foliage light green. A good strong grower which makes an excellent bush shape with little training.

Auntie Jinks (Wilson 1970) Single. Tube pink. Sepals white. Corolla purple. For a basket this one is hard to beat. Flowers continuously and will rapidly fill baskets of any size.

Autumnale (Meteor 1880) Single. Tube and sepals scarlet. Corolla purple. Foliage golden-red. Semi lax

growth. The beauty of the foliage gives a very attractive plant even when not in flower. Although lax in growth the branches tend to grow horizontally.

Baby Blue Eyes (Plummer 1952) Single. Tube and sepals red. Corolla dark lavender. A very strong and floriferous plant which will give service in the hardy border for many years. Foliage medium sized and dark green. Height 4ft (1.2m). Spread 3ft (90cm).

Ballet Girl (Veitch 1894) Double. Tube and sepals bright cerise. Corolla white. Large flowers. Always admired whenever seen. Makes an excellent plant for show purposes.

BAMBINI (Pacey 1985)

Single. Tube and sepals crimson. Corolla mallow. Small flowers. Excellent for growing in window boxes or on a rockery. The small flowers make it an ideal subject for growing in small pots.

Barbara (Tolley 1971) Single. Tube and sepals pale pink. Corolla tangerine-pink. Strong upright grower which will make an excellent standard.

Beacon (Bull 1871) Single. The tube and sepals of this very easy and floriferous hardy fuchsia are deep pink. Corolla bright mauvish pink. The blooms are medium sized and the foliage is darkish green with wavy edges. Height and spread 2ft (60cm).

Beacon Rosa (Burgi-Ott 1972) Sepals red and corolla pink lightly veined with red. The medium-sized blooms are carried on strong upright growing branches. Foliage similar to **Beacon** of which this one is a sport, dark green with wavy edges. Height and spread 2ft (60cm).

Billy Green (Raiser unknown 1966) Single. Tube, sepals and corolla salmon pink. 'Billy Green' is so easy to grow that it should be in everybody's

collection. Will make an excellent plant with a minimum of attention.

Blue Veil (Pacey 1980) Double. Tube pure white. Sepals pure white. Corolla lobelia blue. Large blooms. Strong trailer – will make excellent basket.

Blush of Dawn (Martin 1962) Double. Tube and sepals waxy white. Corolla silver grey/lavender blue. Large flowers. Trailing variety.

BOBBY SHAFTOE (Ryle-Atkinson 1973)

Semi-double. Tube clear frosty white. Sepals clear frosty white flushed with palest pink. Corolla clear frosty white. Profuse flowers of medium size.

BLUE PETER (Porter, M. 1985)

Double. Tube and sepals of this large-flowered plant pinkish white. Corolla imperial purple. Very attractive and eye catching flowers with mid-green foliage.

Bon Accorde (Crousse 1861) Single Tube and sepals white. Corolla pale purple. Upward-looking blooms. Strong upright grower. Grown as a standard it looks very attractive with its flowers growing upwards and away from the foliage.

Brutus (Lemoine 1897) Single. Tube and sepals rich cerise. Corolla dark purple. The richness of the flowers will always enhance a hardy border. One of the earliest to flower and remains so over a long period.

BORDER QUEEN (Ryle/Atkinson 1974)

Single. Tube and sepals rhodamine pink. Corolla pale violet. Very floriferous. Well named and is indeed a queen amongst the border plants. An excellent cultivar to use on the show bench or in the hardy border.

CARL WALLACE (Hobson 1984)

Double. Tube and sepals rosy red. Corolla violet purple. Medium-sized blooms, very free flowering.

CASCADE (Lagen 1937)

Single. Tube and sepals white, heavily flushed with carmine. Corolla deep carmine. An excellent cultivar for use in the basket as its name implies. One fault is that it tends to flower from the very ends of the branches, leaving long expanses of foliage.

Celia Smedley (Bellamy 1970) Single. Tube and sepals neyron rose. Corolla vivid currant red. Large darkish foliage. I make no secret of this being my favourite. The colouring is very distinctive and it will make an excellent upright plant quickly with a minimum of training. Very floriferous.

Chang (Hazard and Hazard 1946) Single. Tube orange red. Sepals orange/red tipped green. Corolla orange. Very floriferous small flowers. The oriental name suits this cultivar well.

Charming (Lye 1895) Single. Tube carmine. Sepals red/cerise. Corolla purple. Foliage yellowish. For the hardy border this one is hard to beat. The colour of the foliage complements the colouring of the flowers. 30in (7cm).

CHECKERBOARD
(Walker and Jones 1948)

Single. Tube carmine. Sepals red shading to white. Corolla red. Strong upright growth. The very distinctive colouring of the flowers makes this cultivar easily recognizable. Its strong upright growth may encourage use as a standard, although the branches can be rather stiff.

Cloverdale Pearl (Gadsby 1974) Single. Tube white. Sepals white/pink tipped with green. Corolla white. An excellent plant for show work or in the border.

Coquet Bell (Ryle-Atkinson 1973) Single to semi-double. Short tube and sepals rose madder. Corolla pale mauve. Bell-shaped blooms with slightly wavy edge. Upright, free-flowering plant.

Coralle (Bonstedt 1905) *Triphylla*-type fuchsia with salmon orange, long, thin tapering tube and sepals. Corolla also salmon orange. Foliage deep sage green and with overall velvety sheen. Growth is upright and very vigorous. The flowers are carried at the ends of the branches.

Cotton Candy (Tiret 1962) Double. Tube white with tinge of pink. Sepals white. Corolla pale pink. Dark to medium green foliage. Rather lax grower and will make good basket.

Countess of Aberdeen (Dobbie-Forbes 1888) Single. Short tube creamy white. Sepals white and slightly upturned. Corolla small and white. Foliage small and medium green. Growth upright and bushy. A superb plant when well grown but is not the easiest of plants to grow as it is prone to botrytis. Does best in semi-shade.

Dark Eyes (Erickson 1958) Double. Tube and sepals deep red. Corolla violet blue. The very attractive deep colouring of this plant – which holds the shape of its double flowers over a long period – makes it an excellent one to grow.

Deep Purple (Garrett 1989) Double. Sepals and tubes white. Corolla dark violet. Foliage medium green. Very strong, spreading and versatile growth helps this large flowered fuchsia to look very attractive when grown in any large hanging container.

Devonshire Dumpling (Hilton 1981) Double. Short thick tube white. Sepals neyron rose and tipped with green. Corolla white with the outer petals flushed with pink. The large flowers are produced in great quantity, and the large white, round buds make the name of this cultivar very appropriate. Medium green foliage. Excellent for growing in large hanging containers.

DISPLAY (Smith 1881)

Single. Tube and sepals rose pink. Corolla deeper rose pink. Saucer-shaped flowers. May be used in any type of growth from small pots to large specimen plants. In the garden it makes a good round mound of flowers. 18in (45cm).

Dollar Princess (Lemoine 1912) Double. Tube and sepals cerise. Corolla rich purple. One of the first to be seen in flower.

Dusky Beauty (Ryle 1981) Single. Tube and sepals neyron rose. Corolla pale purple with pink edges. Small to medium flowers. The beginner on the show bench should try this one. An excellent, easily-shaped plant.

Empress of Prussia (Hoppe 1868) Single. Tube and sepals vivid scarlet. Corolla purple. Plant it and forget it. It will never let you down, growing to its maximum height quickly and producing a constant supply of largish flowers. 36in (90cm).

ESTELLE MARIE (Newton 1973)

Single. Tube and sepals greenish white. Corolla violet. Very attractive colouring on the many flowers produced make this a 'banker' on the show bench. Watch out, though, for flowers which produce more than four sepals.

Flirtation Waltz (Waltz 1962) Double. Tube and sepals creamy-white. Corolla shell pink. An excellent variety which will always produce a good supply of flowers. Care will be needed in transporting to shows as the flowers tend to bruise easily.

Foxtrot (Tolley 1974) Semi-double. Tube and sepals pale cerise. Corolla pale lavender. Use this one in pots or in the garden border. It holds its flowers over a long period.

F. PROCUMBENS (Cunningham 1834)

Tube greenish-yellow, red at base. Sepals green. No corolla. Blue pollen. Growth creeping. Hardy. A native of New Zealand. Seeds, when formed, should be left on the plant and are attractive, being much larger than the very small flowers.

FRANK SAUNDERS (Dyos 1984)

Single. Tube and sepals white. Corolla lilac pink. This cultivar will make a very attractive plant very quickly – always seen on the show benches.

GOLDEN ANNIVERSARY (Stubbs 1980)

Double. Sturdy tube and sepals white. Corolla dark violet ripening to rich ruby red. Young foliage green/gold fading to light green. The natural habit is to spread and the self-branching habit of this cultivar make it ideal for a basket.

Frosted Flame (Handley 1975) Single. Tube and sepals white. Sepals lightly flushed with pink on the inside. Sepals long and narrow and held well out with their tips curling upwards. Corolla bright flame with a deeper edge and pale pink near the base of the petals. Foliage bright green. A natural trailer, this cultivar makes an excellent basket.

Fulgens (De Candolle 1828) Long tube and sepals a light vermillion red. Large lush green leaves. An excellent species for the beginner to try.

Garden News (Handley 1978) Double. Tube and sepals pink. Corolla large and magenta rose. Growth strong, upright and bushy. Foliage medium green. Excellent for the hardy border – usually one of the first to flower from new growth appearing from the base in spring. Height and spread 30–36in (90cm).

Genii (Reiter 1951) Single. Tube and sepals cerise. Corolla rich violet. Foliage yellowish. One of the nicest of hardy plants with its yellow foliage beautifully complementing the richness of its flowers. 30in (75cm).

GOLDEN MARINKA (Weber 1955)

Single. Tube and sepals rich red. Corolla dark red. Foliage green and yellow. Sport from 'Marinka'. An excellent basket variety but a little slow sometimes to get going. Best grown to a reasonable size in pots before placing in the basket.

Happy Anniversary (Raiser and date unknown) Double. Tube, sepals and very full double corolla white. Foliage variegated green and yellow. The growth is naturally trailing so it will make an excellent basket which will be much admired for its large flowers.

Harry Gray (Dunnett 1981) Double. Tube white streaked rose pink. Sepals white. Corolla white/rose pink. Always seen in baskets and half baskets. So floriferous that it is sometimes not possible to see much foliage.

Haute Cuisine (de Graffe 1988) Double. A very attractive colouring on fairly large blooms. Tube and sepals very dark red. Corolla dark aubergine. Foliage medium green on the upper surface but lighter on the lower. The rather lax growth is spreading but strong. This cultivar will make an excellent basket but can also be used as a bush if given some supports.

Hawkshead (Travis 1973) Single. Short tube white with a slight greenish tinge. Sepals white flushed with green, broad and pointed. Barrel-shaped corolla white. Foliage deep green, small with serrated edges. A superb plant for permanent planting in the garden. Height and spread in excess of 3ft (1m).

Heidi Anne (Smith 1969) Double. Tube and sepals crimson. Corolla lilac. An excellent small-flowered double that produces a good symmetrical bush easily.

Herald (Sankey 1867) Single. Tube and sepals scarlet. Corolla deep purple. Foliage light green. A must for the hardy border as the light foliage and the abundance of flowers will always produce an attractive spectacle. 24in (60cm).

Hermiena (Lavieren 1987) Single. Tube and sepals white touched with pink. Corolla dark violet changing to rich plum. A very floriferous cultivar which makes a superb hanging pot or small basket. The foliage is medium green and the plant is very self-branching. Excellent mini-standards have been seen on the show bench.

Jack Shahan (Tiret 1948) Single. Tube and sepals pale rose. Corolla rose bengal. Largish flowers freely produced. Rather lax growth and will make an excellent basket in flower for a long period.

Jenny Sorensen (Wilkinson 1987) Single. Tube and sepals neyron rose. Sepals recurved with green tips. Corolla very pale lilac. Each petal has a distinctive edging of dark violet. As the plant matures the petals become slightly darker with a cerise edging. Foliage flossy medium green. The growth is fairly small but self-branching and upright. Will make an eye-catching small standard.

Joan Goy (Webb 1989) Single. Tube and sepals white blushed pink with recurved tips. Corolla lilac pink maturing to light lilac pink. The open bell shaped flowers are half flared and are carried in an erect position. Foliage dark shiny green. Growth is short jointed and self-branching.

Joan Smith (Thorne 1958) Single. Tube and sepals pink. Corolla pink/cerise. Excellent strong upright grower.

Joy Patmore (Turner 1961) Single. Tube and sepals waxy white. Corolla rich carmine. You will rarely find a show where this cultivar does not appear. The pastel shading of its flowers produced on an easily-shaped plant makes it a 'banker' for the showmen.

King's Ransom (Schnabel 1954) Double. Tube and sepals white. Corolla purple. A striking flower which is freely produced on a strong growing bush.

La Campanella (Blackwell 1968) Semi-double. Tube and sepals white/pink. Corolla purple. A must for the users of baskets. Perpetually in flower and self-cleaning. Will take full sunlight. A slow starter when first struck as a cutting but makes up for lost time later.

Lady Isobel Barnett (Gadsby 1968) Single. Tube and sepals rose. Corolla rose purple. One of the most floriferous cultivars. If it has a fault it is that it produces too many flowers. Six to eight from each leaf axil is not unusual. Nevertheless an excellent cultivar.

LADY PATRICIA MOUNTBATTEN
(Clark 1985)

Single. Tube and sepals palest pink. Corolla pale lilac. The delicate colouring of this cultivar makes it very attractive. Will be seen on the show benches for a long time to come.

LORD LONSDALE
(Raiser and date unknown)

Single. Tube and sepals light apricot. Corolla orange peach. The very attractive flowers are of medium size. The foliage is light green and has the unfortunate habit of curling. Growth is rather lax. Not the easiest of plants to grow.

Lady Thumb (Roe 1966) Semi-double. Tube and sepals carmine. Corolla white. Sport of 'Tom Thumb'. For the border, the window box or patio display, this one is a must. The family – 'Tom Thumb', 'Son of Thumb', and 'Lady Thumb' – are essential for the front of the hardy border. 12in (30cm).

Lena (Bunney 1862) Semi-double. Tube and sepals flesh pink. Corolla rosy magenta flushed pink and paling at base. Growth lax bush and will make an excellent basket. Hardy. 18in (45cm).

Liebriez (Kohene 1874) Semi-double. Tube and sepals pale cerise. Corolla pinkish white. Continuous blooming. Excellent for all pot work or as a hardy plant in the garden.

Loeky (de Graaf 1981) Single. Tube and sepals rosy red. Corolla lavender fading to rose pink. Medium-sized, flat, saucer-shaped flowers.

Love's Reward (Bambridge 1986) Single. The small to medium-sized flowers are produced in great quantity throughout the season. Tube and sepals white. Corolla violet blue. Foliage medium green. Growth is short and self-branching. A superb plant for the smaller pots on the show bench.

Madame Cornelissen (Cornelissen 1860) Single to semi-double. Tube and sepals rich scarlet. Corolla white veined with cerise. The smallish flowers are freely produced throughout the season. Foliage dark green. Growth is strong, upright and bushy. Worth trying as a hedge. Height and spread 24–30in (60–75cm).

Malibu Mist (Stubbs 1985) Double. Short tube white. Sepals held horizontally, white on the upper side and white tinged with pink on the lower. Corolla opens blue violet streaked with light pink and matures to cyclamen purple, with white at the base of each petal. Foliage medium green. Growth is lax and it will make a basket or a bush if given supports.

MARCUS GRAHAM (Stubbs 1985)

Double. Tube and sepals salmon or pink. Corolla delicate shade of salmon. Foliage medium green. Growth is very strong and most suitable for large bushes or standards.

Margaret Pilkington (Clark 1984) Single. Tube and sepals waxy white/pink. Corolla bishop's violet. An eye-catching cultivar.

Margaret Roe (Gadsby 1968) Single. Tube and sepals rosy red. Corolla pale violet-purple. Very free medium blooms held erect from the plant. Strong upright growth.

Marilyn Olsen (Wilkinson 1987) Single. Tube and sepals rosy pink. Corolla almost white. Very floriferous and rapidly became a favourite among the showmen.

MARGARET BROWN (Wood 1949)

Single. Tube and sepals rose pink. Corolla light rose. Very prolific flowerer, and one I would always recommend. Throughout the summer plants of this cultivar drip with flowers. 24in (60cm).

MARIN GLOW (Reedstrom 1954)

Single. Tube and sepals waxy white. Corolla rich purple. The distinctive colouring of this cultivar will always cause it to be popular with all who see it. Easy to grow and train.

Marinka (Rozaine-Doucharlat 1902) Single. Tube and sepals rich red. Corolla darker red. The standard by which other basket variety fuchsias are measured. The rich red of its flowers contrasts beautifully with the dark green of its leaves.

Mary (Bonstedt 1894) Single. Tube, sepals and corolla vivid scarlet. Rich dark sage green foliage. Very free-flowering. Upright growth. An excellent one to use for *Triphylla* classes.

Mieke Meursing (Hopwood 1968) Single to semi-double. Tube and sepals red. Corolla pale pink veined red. Very floriferous, easily-shaped plant. This cultivar has been one of the most successful winners on the show bench since it was introduced. (The anxiety of knowing whether this one should be classified as single or semi-double on the show bench has been removed, as singles and semi-doubles can now be shown in the same class.)

Minirose (de Graffe 1983) Single. Tube and sepals pale rose. Corolla dark rose. The smallness of the flowers make this an excellent variety for use in small pots. Flowers continuously over a very long period.

Mipam (Gubler 1976) Single. Tube and sepals pale carmine. Corolla magenta pink. Grown as a bush or shrub this plant will provide you with a perpetual bouquet of flowers.

Mrs Lovell Swisher (Evans and Reeves 1942) Single. Tube and sepals flesh pink. Corolla deep rose. This strong upright grower always produces vast quantities of medium to small flowers.

Natasha Sinton (Sinton 1990) Double. Tube and sepals orchid pink. Corolla orchid pink veined with magenta. The flowers are of medium size and are freely produced. Foliage mid green and the natural growth is as a trailer.

Nellie Nuttall (Roe 1977) Single. Tube and sepals bright red. Corolla white. For small pot work there is no better plant to use – the brilliance of its flowers makes it shine. Easily trained into all shapes.

OTHER FELLOW
(Hazard and Hazard 1946)

Single. Tube and sepals waxy white. Corolla coral pink. Many small flowers make this an extremely attractive plant.

Orange Crush (Handley 1972) Single. Tube and sepals and corolla orange salmon. If you like the orange colours, this one must be on your list. An excellent variety which flowers over a long period. Try it out of doors.

Pacquesa (Clyne 1974) Single/semi-double. Tube and sepals deep red. Corolla white. With its fairly large flowers freely produced this cultivar is always seen gracing the show bench.

Patio Princess (Sinton 1988) Double. Tube and sepals neyron rose. Corolla white veined with rose. Foliage medium green. The natural growth is upright, self-branching and bushy. This cultivar will make an excellent plant for a patio tub.

Paula Jane (Tite 1975) Semi-double. Tube and sepals carmine rose. Corolla beetroot-purple maturing to ruby red. Good strong floriferous grower.

Perky Pink (Erickson-Lewis 1959) Double. Tube and sepals pink. Corolla white/pink. The medium-sized blooms are freely produced. Does well in the show class category.

Perry Park (Handley 1977) Single. Tube and sepals pale pink. Corolla bright rose. The medium-sized flowers are produced early in the season. This is a very floriferous cultivar bearing as many as six flowers in each leaf axil.

Pink Galore (Fuchsia-La 1958) Double. Tube, sepals and corolla candy pink. Dark foliage. Always sought as a good basket variety. As the individual plants are not of great size it is worth considering placing more than the usual number of plants in each basket.

Pink Marshmallow (Stubbs 1971) Double. Tube and sepals pale pink. Corolla white. Large flowers. A basket of this cultivar is very eye-catching. The large flowers are freely produced and cascade beautifully.

Pixie (Russell 1960) Single. Tube and sepals cerise. Corolla rosy mauve, foliage slightly yellowish. The vigorous growth will rapidly form an excellent bush in the garden. Can be used for hedge work if required. One of the nicest varieties. 30in (75cm).

President Leo Boullemier (Burns 1983) Single. Short fluted tube streaked magenta. Sepals white. Corolla magenta blue maturing to blush pink. Medium-sized blooms. Excellent for temporary use in the hardy border.

PINK FANTASIA (Webb 1989)

Single. Tube and sepals of this superb cultivar are bright pink or red. Corolla fluorescent violet to mauve. Foliage medium to darker green. The flowers are produced mainly at the ends of the branches and are upward looking. The flowers are produced in great profusion throughout the season.

PRESIDENT MARGARET SLATER
(Taylor 1972)

Single. Tube and sepal white. Corolla mauve/pink. Although rather late to come into flower this cultivar makes an excellent basket. Tends to flower at the ends of the branches but, if layered so that branches lie on

President Stanley J Wilson (Thorne 1968) Single. Tube and sepals cerise. Corolla rose carmine. The flowers are produced on long stalks and hang beautifully. An excellent basket produced from this cultivar is a sight to behold.

Quasar (Walker 1974) Double. Tube white, medium length. Sepals white. Corolla violet, shaded white at the base of each petal. The flowers are medium to large sized and the blooms are very compact. Foliage light green. Growth is naturally trailing and will make a superb basket.

Rose Fantasia (Wilkinson 1991) Single. This sport from **Pink Fantasia** has tube and sepals which are deep pink. Corolla pink with a hint of mauve. Foliage medium green. Growth is upright, self-branching and bushy. The flowers are held horizontally or higher.

Royal Velvet (Waltz 1962) Double. Tube and sepals crimson. Corolla deep purple. Large flowers but floriferous for size. Always greatly admired whenever seen. The large double flowers are produced far more abundantly than is usual for this size of flower.

Rufus (Nelson 1952) Single. Tube and sepals and corolla bright red (sometimes referred to as 'Rufus the Red'). Strong upright grower. Very easy to grow and to shape. Will never let you down and the brightness of the flowers gives a fluorescent effect. 30in (75cm).

Salmon Cascade (Bielby/Oxtoby 1991) Single. Tube dark salmon. Sepals pale pink shading to white and tipped with green. Corolla deep orange red. Foliage fairly large and medium green. The growth is naturally trailing and it will therefore make an excellent basket.

Saturnus (de Groot 1970) Single. Tube and sepals red. Corolla light purple. The small flowers abundantly produced make this an excellent cultivar to use in small pots. Very eye-catching.

Snowcap (Henderson 1890) Semi-double. Tube and sepals bright red. Corolla pure white. Strong grower. Many people have a great affection for this cultivar – the clearness of the red and the white always makes it stand out. Easy to train and to shape. One of the first cultivars I grew, and I would never be without it. 18–24in (45–60cm).

Son of Thumb (Gubler 1978) Semi-double. Tube and sepals cerise. Corolla lilac. Sport from 'Tom Thumb'. For the front of a border or for use in a window box this, together with 'Tom Thumb' and 'Lady Thumb', is a must. Will produce a well-shaped low bush very quickly. 12in (30cm).

Stanley Cash (Pennisi 1970) Double. Tube and sepals white tipped green. Corolla dark royal purple. Large flowers freely produced which hold their shape well over a long period. An excellent basket variety.

String of Pearls (Pacey 1976) Single to semi-double. Tube and sepals pale rose. Corolla pale purple. Beautifully named and very descriptive of its method

SWINGTIME (Tiret 1950)

Double. Tube and sepals red. Corolla sparkling white. A basket variety par excellence. Perhaps the most popular of all for growing in baskets, although the growth can be rather stiff and therefore does not trail quite as easily as some. By weighting the ends of the laterals in the early stages of growth, the necessary trailing qualities can be utilized.

of growth. The pearl-like flowers hang like tassels along the branches and are extremely attractive.

Taddle (Gubler 1974) Single. Tube and sepals deep rose pink. Corolla waxy white. A well-formed bush of this cultivar can easily be grown. The quantity of flowers produced over a long season will always make this a very popular variety.

Thalia (Bonstêdt 1905) Single. Tube, sepals and corolla orange/scarlet. Dark foliage with purple underneath. *Triphylla* type, and one of the easiest and best. 'Thalia' tends to retain its leaves lower down better than others. Very often seen with a winning card on the show bench.

Ting-a-Ling (Schnabel-Paskeson 1959) Tube, sepals and corolla white. Saucer-shaped flowers. The purity of white is always present and the flowers are freely produced.

TENNESSEE WALTZ
(Walker and Jones 1951)

Double. Tube and sepals rose. Corolla lilac. No garden should be without this one. Excellent in the centre of a border, and will repay with flowers over a long period. 20in (50cm).

TOM THUMB (Baudinat 1850)

Single. Tube and sepals carmine. Corolla mauve veined carmine. Small flowers extremely free. Excellent for the front of the hardy border or in window boxes. Grow with 'Lady Thumb' and 'Son of Thumb', its two sports. 12in (30cm).

TRUMPETER (Reiter 1946)

Triphylla. The long and thick tubes are pale geranium lake. The sepals, which are short and pointed, are of the same colouring. The corolla is also geranium lake and the petals are short and fairly compact. The long blooms darken as the flower matures. The foliage is bluish green. The flowers are carried on long wiry stems. Naturally trailing in its habit, this triphylla type will make a good basket.

Tom West (Meillez 1853) single. Tube and sepals red. Corolla purple. Foliage green/white/red. Excellent plant for variegated foliage. It will make an excellent well-shaped plant quite easily. Few flowers are produced, but as these are not required when exhibiting 'foliage' plants this is no drawback.

Torvill and Dean (Pacey 1985) Double. Tube pale cerise. Sepals pale cerise, tipped green. Corolla almost pure white. Large blooms, which are freely produced.

Waveney Gem (Burns 1985) Single. Tube and sepals white. Corolla pink. Very floriferous. One of the numerous 'Waveney' cultivars, all of which are very well worth growing. This one can be used for upright pot work or in baskets. Flowers continu-

ously over a very long period and is always much admired.

Winston Churchill (Garson 1942) Double. Tube and sepals pink. Corolla lavender blue. Another show stopper. The double flowers, which are medium to large, are freely produced on a plant which is easily shaped. Not the easiest to get through the winter but new plants can be grown from early season cuttings and will flower profusely.

Societies and Shows

To obtain the greatest amount of satisfaction from your enthusiasm for growing fuchsias I would strongly recommend that you consider joining either a society local to you or the national society, preferably both.

National societies are responsible for organizing shows in various parts of the country and produce regular publications which are of considerable interest. It is very encouraging to know that, as a result of your membership, you have available to you the expertise of many people able and willing to answer any queries that you may have. Naturally the national societies sometime appear to be rather remote because of distances but this should not be too great a drawback as communication with the society officials can often bring you in touch with other like-minded individuals in your immediate area.

The local societies are able to offer considerable assistance and it will be possible to attend regular instructional and informative meetings and to enjoy the company of others who share your interests. Many long-lasting friendships have been formed as a result of introductions made at such meetings.

I will not attempt to include names and addresses of secretaries of national or local societies as these often change. However it is possible to obtain such addresses by enquiring at local libraries (for your local society address) and by perusing the pages of gardening magazines for details of shows and perhaps the secretary's name for the national society.

It is my pleasure to visit many of the local societies around the United Kingdom and I have always been struck by the friendship and camaraderie that exists. Yes, there will be a competitive element when the annual show is staged but such rivalry and desire to improve upon one's own previous entries is bound to be healthy. Many societies prefer to stage annual fuchsia displays of a non-competitive type, which give members the opportunity to bring along any plants which have given them considerable satisfaction in the growing. Not all plants make good show specimens – many have minds of their own and do not believe in growing with any sense of symmetry. Such plants will still make a very colourful display when shown, en masse, with many others. Such displays are also often used as a means of raising funds for local charitable causes, a very worthwhile and satisfying object.

So, being interested in fuchsias, I would strongly recommend that you seek out like-minded individuals and join them if they are already part of a local society or, if one has not yet been formed in your area, why not consider taking the first steps and start one. Good luck.

Glossary

Anther The pollen-bearing part of the stamen.

Axil The angle formed by the junction of leaf and stem from which new shoots or flowers develop.

Berry The fleshy fruit containing the seeds; the ovary after fertilization.

Biennial The process of growing a plant one year to flower the following year.

Bleeding The loss of sap from a cut or damaged shoot of a plant.

Break To branch or send out new growth from dormant wood.

Bud Undeveloped shoot found in axils of plants – also the developing flower.

Calyx The sepals and tube together, the outer part of the flower.

Cambium A layer of activity dividing cells around the xylem or wood.

Chromosome Bodies consisting of a series of different genes arranged in linear fashion. They occur in the nucleus of every plant cell.

Clear stem The amount of stem free of all growth. It is measured from the soil level to the first branch or leaf. It is of importance when growing standards or bushes.

Compost A mixture of differing ingredients specially prepared for the growing of cuttings, plant or the sowing of seed.

Cordate Heart-shaped.

Corolla The collective term for the petals, the inner part of the flower.

Cultivar A cultivated variety, a cross between two hybrids or species and a hybrid. Normally written 'cv'.

Cutting A piece from a plant encouraged to form roots and thus produce a new plant. This is vegetative reproduction and plants produced by this method are true to the parental type.

Cyme An inflorescence where the central flower opens first as in *F. arborescens*.

Damp down Raise the humidity of the atmosphere in the greenhouse by spraying plants, benches or paths with water.

Damping off The collapse and possible death of cuttings or seedlings, usually due to attack at ground level by soil-borne fungi.

Double A fuchsia with eight or more petals.

Emasculation The process of removing immature stamens from a host plant to prevent self-pollination, during the cross-pollination of two plants.

Feeding Applying additional plant nutrients to the compost in an effort to enhance growth or remedy compost deficiencies.

Fertilization The union of male and female cells.

Fibrous roots Thin white roots produced from

'Geoff Barnet'.

the main fleshy roots vital for the taking up of water and nutrients essential for healthy growth.

Filament The stalk of the stamens.

Final stop The last removal of the 'growing tip' which a plant received before being allowed to grow to flowering stage.

First stop The removal of the growing tip of a rooted cutting to encourage branching into the required shape.

Frost protection Maintaining a temperature above freezing point (32°F; 0°C).

Half hardy Plants which may be bedded out during the summer but will need frost protection during the winter months.

Hardy Plants that can be permanently planted in the garden.

Hybrid A cross between two species.

Hypanthium The correct term for the tube.

Internode The portion of stem between two 'nodes'. Rooting from this section is described as 'internodal'.

Lanceolate Lance-, or spear-shaped.

Leaf axil The point at which the leaf joins the stem and from which the side shoots will be produced.

Leaf node The slightly swollen area from which the leaf grows from the stem.

Mutation 'Sport' departure from the normal parent type.

N.A.S. The abbreviation used by show judges to indicate that an entry in a class is 'Not According to Schedule'. Exhibits so marked cannot be considered for an award within the show.

Node Part of the stem from which a leaf or a bud arises. When taking cuttings, roots form most readily from this point.

Nutrients The food used by the plant from the growing medium necessary for the sustaining of healthy growth.

Ornamental foliage.

Ornamental A term used to describe those plants which have decorative foliage. The foliage can be variegated or of a colour other than the usual green.

Ovary The part containing the ovules which, after fertilization, swells and encloses the seeds.

Over-wintering The storage of plants during the resting period of the plants, the winter months, so that the tissue remains alive though dormant.

Ovate Egg-shaped.

Pedicel The flower stalk.

Petal A division of the corolla.

Petaloid Smaller outer petal of the corolla.

Petiole The leaf stalk.

Photosynthesis The process carried out by the plant in the manufacture of plant food from water and carbon dioxide, using the energy absorbed by chlorophyll from sunlight.

Pinch To remove the growing tips.

Pistil The female part of the flower, consisting of the ovary, stigma and style.

Pot-bound When the plant container is full of roots to such an extent that the plant will become starved of nutrients.

Pot back To remove the old compost from around the roots of a plant, replacing the plant in fresh compost and a smaller-sized pot.

Pot on To transfer the plant from one size of pot to a larger one, so that there will be a continuation in the supply of nutrients.

Potting up Transferring a seedling or rooted cutting from its initial seed box or propagator into a plant pot.

Propagation Increasing of stock by means of seeds or by rooting cuttings.

Pruning The shortening of laterals or roots to enhance the shape of the plant or remove damaged portions.

Re-potting Removing a plant from its pot, shaking off as much of the old compost as possible without damaging the roots, and replacing it, usually in the same size of pot and using fresh compost.

'Alison Ewart' will make a beautiful miniature standard, and is an ideal exhibition plant.

Rubbing out The removal of unwanted side growths (for example, on a standard stem), usually in early bud stage.

Scar The 'scab' formed during the healing process of a cut surface. Forms at the end of a cutting before rooting commences.

Self-pollination The transference of pollen from anther to stigma of the same flower or another flower on the same plant.

Semi-double A fuchsia with five, six or seven petals.

Sepals Normally four, which with the tube form the calyx, the outermost part of the flower.

Shading Exclusion of some of the rays of the sun with blinds, netting or a glass colourant.

Shaping To grow a plant into a definite shape by means of training the laterals or by selective pinching out of the growing tips.

Siblings Offspring of the same female and male parents.

Single A fuchsia with four petals only.

Species Plants which are recognizably distinct occurring in the wild and which will breed true from seed.

Sport A shoot differing in character from the typical growth of the parent plant, often giving rise to a new cultivar, and which must be propagated vegetatively.

Stamen The male part of the flower, comprising the filament and anther.

Stigma The part of the pistil to which the pollen grain adheres.

Stop To remove the growing tip.

The style and the anthers.

Striking a cutting The insertion of a prepared cutting into a suitable rooting compost.

Style The stalk carrying the stigma.

Systemics Insecticides or fungicides that are taken up by the roots and carried into the sap of a plant, thus causing it to become poisonous to sucking insects or protected from the attack of viruses. It can also be absorbed through the foliage if applied in spray form.

Trace elements Nutrients required by a plant to maintain steady and healthy growth (boron, copper, manganese, molybdenum and zinc).

Transpiration Loss of water, mainly from the surface of the leaves.

Tube The elongated part of the calyx, correctly called the hypanthium.

Turgid The condition of the plant cells after absorption of water to full capacity.

Turning The term used to describe the turning of the plant daily in an effort to achieve balanced growth from all directions.

Variety Botanically a variant of the species, but formerly used to denote what is now commonly called a cultivar.

Virus An agent causing systemic disease too small to be seen other than with powerful microscopes, but transmitted very easily.

Whip A term given to a single stem of a plant that is being grown with a view to producing a 'standard'.

Wilt The drooping of a plant, usually as a result of lack of moisture within the plant. Can be caused by disease or toxins.

Woody growth Stems of a plant that have become thickened and brown with age. Particularly noticeable at the base of the plant.

Index